I0015060

Artificial Intelligence (AI) in Patent Practice: No Patent Attorneys Were Harmed in the Making of this AI Revolution

Dr. Roberto Rosas and Juan Vasquez,Esq.

Co-authors: Dianisa Erica Sosa,
Francisco Javier Hernandez-Rodriguez and Daniel Kovach

outskirts
press

Abstract

Artificial Intelligence (AI) in Patent Practice: No Patent Attorneys Were Harmed in the Making of this AI Revolution provides a comprehensive examination of the rapidly evolving role of artificial intelligence (AI) in the patent law profession. Rather than a traditional legal text, this work offers an in-depth exploration of the profound impacts AI will have on patent attorneys' workflows and practices.

The central inquiry posits whether AI will ultimately replace patent attorneys or serve as a powerful complementary technology. This study contends that AI is poised to become an indispensable tool that augments and enhances the patent attorney's capabilities rather than renders them obsolete. Through detailed analysis of a patent attorney's typical workweek utilizing AI assistance, the text illustrates how tedious tasks that formerly demanded significant temporal investments can be dramatically expedited. Patent searches, drafting, prosecution, and opinion work are all demonstrated to be vastly more efficient when conducted with the aid of AI's processing power and aptitude.

However, the work extends beyond a purely instrumentalist perspective, also weighing the risks of AI misapplication and the potential for unintended consequences. Thought-provoking discussion highlights how AI's misunderstandings can occasionally produce absurd or unintended outcomes that must be carefully monitored by human oversight. Simultaneously, the innovative possibilities of using AI to enliven dense patent filings with greater clarity and narrative engagement are examined.

Ultimately, the text argues for an emerging collaborative relationship between AI systems and patent attorneys as a potent force for protecting intellectual property rights in the modern era. Legal professionals, inventors, technologists, and theorists alike will find value in this authoritative contribution exploring AI's frontiers in the patent law domain. As AI continues advancing, this work provides vital insights into how it can be effectively leveraged to drive innovation while safeguarding creators' interests.

Biographies

AUTHORS

Dr. Roberto Rosas is a Distinguished Research Professor of Law at St. Mary's University School of Law in San Antonio, Texas, where he was awarded the Distinguished Faculty Award from the St. Mary's University Alumni Association, as well as a *Profesor Externo* (External Professor) in the J.S.D. program with the Universidad de Guadalajara. He earned his B.S. in electromechanical engineering and later his J.D. from the Universidad de Guadalajara, Mexico, and his Doctor of Juridical Science (J.S.D.) -the highest law degree- at the Universidad Europea de Madrid, Spain. He was recently designated Distinguished Research Professor of Law Emeritus for St. Mary's University.

Dr. Rosas gives special thanks to Dr. Kenia Yasbeth Aguilar Cisneros, Director of the Law Firm Grupo Lex, and her research assistant Alejandro Mondragón Tielve, for their invaluable help in the research and contributions to this book.

Juan Vasquez, a patent attorney with Whitaker Chalk Swindle & Schwartz, combines an Electrical Engineering background and Air Force experience to specialize in patent law. Co-founder of virtuaPatent, he's pioneering AI's role in streamlining patent services. With over a decade in the field, Juan's expertise bridges technology and intellectual property law, positioning him as a key resource for innovators seeking to protect their advancements in today's fast-evolving tech landscape. Contact at: Juan.Vasquez@virtuaPatent.com.

CO-AUTHORS

Dianisa Erica Sosa graduated from St. Mary's University School of Law in the Spring of 2023. She also holds a master's degree from New Mexico State University in Criminal Justice with a minor in Public Administration. She has helped and aided Dr. Roberto Rosas as a research assistant since 2021 and has aided him in numerous of his published works.

Francisco Javier Hernandez-Rodriguez graduated from St. Mary's University School of Law in Spring 2024 in San Antonio, Texas. BA in Political Science from St. Edward's University in Austin, Texas.

Daniel Kovach, cofounder of virtuaPatent, is a highly accomplished AI and Machine Learning specialist. He holds a master's degree in applied mathematics and dual Bachelor's degrees in Mathematics and Physics from Florida Institute of Technology. He currently serves as a Financial Services consultant, producing enterprise-level solutions with C-level visibility for Fortune 500 companies such as Citibank and Synchrony.

Foreword

As we stand at the cusp of a technological renaissance, where artificial intelligence (AI) begins to weave its threads through the fabric of patent law, this book, *Artificial Intelligence (AI) in Patent Practice: No Patent Attorneys Were Harmed in the Making of this AI Revolution* offers a timely and insightful exploration of how AI is transforming the practice of patent law, augmenting the capabilities of patent attorneys, and ushering in a future of unparalleled efficiency and innovation. Crafted at the intersection of innovation and jurisprudence, it aims to demystify the future landscape of patent attorneys—a profession steeped in tradition yet on the cusp of transformation.

The authors, led by the esteemed Dr. Roberto Rosas and the seasoned patent attorney Juan Vasquez, provide a comprehensive and engaging narrative that delves into the intricacies of AI's integration into patent practice. Drawing from their extensive expertise and foresight, they paint a vivid picture of a future where AI and human expertise converge, enabling patent attorneys to navigate the complexities of intellectual property with unprecedented precision and strategic acumen.

The journey within these pages is not just a narrative; it's an expedition into the heart of how AI promises to augment, rather than supplant, the intellect and intuition of patent attorneys. Through a meticulously curated exploration, we traverse the implications of AI's integration into patent practice, navigating through patent searches, drafting, prosecution, and the nuanced art of opinion work. Yet, it's imperative to underscore that this exploration is a glimpse into a future not fully realized. The scenarios and reflections presented are forward-looking, envisioning a world where AI's potential is harnessed to elevate the practice of patent law to unprecedented heights.

In crafting this book, we sought not just to chart the theoretical synergies between patent attorneys and AI but to ground these projections in the real-world context of their work. The narrative unfolds through the lens of a reimagined week in the life of a patent attorney—transformed yet familiar. This vantage point offers a unique perspective, illuminating the practical, day-to-day enhancements that AI brings to the fore, from efficiency gains to qualitative leaps in the work produced.

This forward vision of the patent attorney, empowered by AI, does not diminish their role but instead heralds a new era of strategic insight and creative problem-solving. It posits a future where the depth of human expertise and the breadth of artificial intelligence converge, crafting a partnership that transcends the limitations of either working in isolation. In this envisioned future, patent attorneys are not relics of a bygone era but pioneers on the frontier of intellectual property law, steering the helm of innovation with AI as their compass.

As you delve into the chapters that follow, bear in mind that this book is both a reflection on the potential of AI in patent law and a call to embrace the transformative power of technology. It is a narrative that invites patent attorneys, technologists, and innovators alike to envision their roles within this evolving landscape—to see beyond the horizon of current practice and towards the limitless possibilities that await.

And in a delightful twist, the foreword you're reading now? Crafted by AI itself—a testament to the advances we've made with language models. Who better to introduce a book on the future of AI in patent law than an AI? Fear not, we haven't yet learned how to play golf or enjoy a sunset, so your jobs are safe for now. This demonstration of

AI's capabilities in language and thought synthesis is but a taste of the collaborative potential that lies ahead.

Welcome to a journey of discovery, where AI and the art of patent law merge to redefine the contours of intellectual property protection. Welcome to the future, eloquently introduced by one of its architects.

Table of Contents

Introduction

In the ever-evolving landscape of intellectual property (IP) law, understanding its intricacies is paramount for safeguarding creative and innovative endeavors. Included in the Constitution under Article 1, IP protections serve "To promote the Progress of Science and useful Arts, by securing for limited Times to Authors and Inventors the exclusive Right to their respective Writings and Discoveries." IP law encompasses a broad spectrum of legal principles and regulations designed to protect intangible assets such as inventions, artistic works, trademarks, and trade secrets.

The components of IP law span across several key areas, including copyright, patents, trademarks, and other intellectual assets. Copyright law grants rights such as distribution and reproduction among others, to creators of original works. Trademark law safeguards brands and their associated symbols or phrases, ensuring consumers can identify and distinguish products and services. A patent, the main focus of our discussion herein, is an exclusive right granted to an individual for an invention of their creation. The exclusive right grants the patent holder the ability to exclude others from making, selling, or reproducing the invention.

As technology continues to advance at an unprecedented pace, new tools and methodologies emerge to aid in navigating the complexities of IP law. Up-and-coming technologies such as blockchain and machine learning hold promise in revolutionizing how IP rights are managed and enforced. Furthermore, AI is rapidly transforming the legal landscape by providing innovative solutions to streamline processes and improve accessibility. AI-powered legal tools, such as contract review systems and predictive analytics software, empower legal professionals to efficiently analyze vast amounts of data, identify patterns, and make informed decisions. Applied to patent law, AI can be used to compare the patent idea to prior art in order to detect similarities and minimize potential infringements. Moreover, the ability to cut times in patent applications allows for the system to be more widely available to the masses. Attorneys would take less time, and in turn, charge less to clients, allowing for a larger demographic than ever before to take advantage of the protections afforded to them for their new ideas and inventions.

The impact of AI extends beyond the legal sector, permeating various business sectors and revolutionizing traditional practices. By automating routine tasks, AI enhances productivity, reduces costs, and enables organizations to focus on strategic initiatives. In industries ranging from healthcare and finance to manufacturing and retail, AI-backed technologies are optimizing operations, driving innovation, and delivering personalized experiences to consumers.

In essence, the convergence of IP law and emerging technologies such as AI heralds a new era of innovation, accessibility, and efficiency. By embracing these advancements, legal professionals can navigate the complexities of IP law with greater ease and allow the process of patent applications to be a smoother and more efficient task for both the client and attorney.

In the coming chapters, we will explore, as we stand on the brink of a transformative era where AI is poised to redefine the traditional roles and tasks of patent attorneys, the fascinating integration of AI into the core functions of a patent attorney's work. We will explore how this cutting-edge technology not only augments the capabilities of patent attorneys but also streamlines the intricate processes involved in protecting intellectual property.

In the coming chapters, we will see the tireless efforts, meticulous analysis, and strategic insight that patent attorneys invest in serving their clients. The dedication to safeguarding innovation demands not just legal acumen but also a significant investment of time and effort. However, as we stand on the cusp of a new digital dawn, AI emerges as a powerful ally, capable of performing complex analyses, sifting through vast datasets, and providing insights at a speed and scale unfathomable to the human mind.

As we explore this, we'll also consider how the role of patent attorneys will evolve in an AI-enhanced future. Far from rendering the human element obsolete, AI will enable attorneys to focus on the most strategic aspects of their work, leveraging their unique insights and creativity to guide clients through the complex landscape of intellectual property law with unparalleled precision and foresight.

Join us as we embark on a journey through the possibilities and promises of AI in revolutionizing the way patent attorneys contribute to the world of innovation, illustrating a future where technology and human expertise converge to protect and promote the progress of human ingenuity.

1

Here Comes the Patent Attorney

In the world of legal professions, specializing in a particular area of the law is not just a pathway taken by most lawyers, but indeed a necessity for becoming an effective practitioner. Like many other professions, the Law branches into various specialties, each requiring a unique set of skills and knowledge. Among these specialties, patent law stands out as a field where legal acumen intersects with technological innovation.

Patent law plays a pivotal role in fostering innovation and driving the economy. Patents provide legal protection for inventions, encouraging inventors and companies to develop new technologies and products.[1] This legal framework is essential for innovation, ensuring that creators can benefit from their inventions without fear of unauthorized replication. Patent law is distinct in its combination of legal principles with technical understanding. It is not merely about understanding the law; it is about comprehending the intricacies of inventions, technological advancements, and how they align with legal protections. This blend of knowledge areas creates a fascinating and challenging career path, which leads to the emergence of the patent attorney.

Patent attorneys are key players in this ecosystem. They ensure that the legal rights of inventors and companies are secured, providing

---

1   *Patent Essentials*, UNITED STATES PATENT AND TRADEMARK OFFICE, https://www.uspto.gov/patents/basics/essentials#questions.

a pathway for new technologies to move from concept to market. Without patent attorneys, the bridge between invention and legal protection would be challenging to navigate, potentially stifling innovation and economic growth.

How did the Patent Attorney Come to Be?

The journey of patent attorneys began centuries ago, rooted in the burgeoning recognition of inventors' rights and the need to protect the fruits of human ingenuity. The genesis of patent attorneys is intertwined with the history of patents themselves. The concept of granting exclusive rights to inventors can be traced back to ancient Greece, but it was during the Renaissance in Italy that the modern patent system began to take shape.[2] However, the role of the patent attorney, as a specialized legal advocate dedicated to navigating the complexities of patent law, did not emerge until much later.

In the 19th century, as the Industrial Revolution reached its zenith, the explosion of inventions and the consequent rise in patent applications necessitated a more structured system for protecting intellectual property. Countries began to formalize their patent laws, and with this, the need for experts who could navigate these laws became evident.[3] It was within this context that the patent attorney profession was born, initially in England and soon after in the United States and other parts of the world.

The earliest patent attorneys were often scientists or engineers who, recognizing the legal challenges inventors faced, sought legal

---

2   Stefano Comino, Alberto Galasso, Clara Graziano, *The Diffusion of New Institution: Evidence from Renaissance Venice's Patent System*, NATIONAL BUREAU OF ECONOMIC RESEARCH (Dec. 2017), https://www.nber.org/system/files/working_papers/w24118/w24118.pdf.

3   Joel Mokyr, *Intellectual Property Rights, the Industrial Revolution, and the Beginnings of Modern Economic Growth*, 99 AER 349, 349-355 (2009) (Importance of patent system to the promotion of innovation in Britain).

qualifications to better assist in protecting inventions. Their unique blend of technical expertise and legal acumen made them invaluable allies to inventors. They were not just lawyers; they were translators, translating the complex language of patents into a form that could be understood and protected within the legal system. [4]

As the 20th century progressed, the role of the patent attorney continued to evolve and expand, shaped by the relentless pace of technological innovation and the increasingly global nature of intellectual property protection. Today, patent attorneys are more than just guardians of individual inventions; they are strategists, helping to navigate the intricate web of global patents, and advocates, defending the rights of inventors in an ever-changing technological landscape.[5]

The story of patent attorneys is a testament to the enduring importance of protecting intellectual property. As we delve deeper into their role, from the initial drafting of a patent application to the complex negotiations of patent litigation, we gain a deeper appreciation for the pivotal role they play in fostering innovation and protecting the rights of inventors.

What is a Patent Attorney?

But what exactly is a patent attorney? In simple terms, a patent attorney is a legal expert specializing in patent law.[6] The role of a patent attorney encompasses a variety of tasks, from advising on patentability to drafting and prosecuting patent applications.[7] Unlike general practice attorneys, patent attorneys dive deep into the technical details of

---

4   Kara W. Swanson, *The Emergence of the Professional Patent Practitioner*, 50 T & C 519, 530-531 (2009) (Early practitioners and their backgrounds within patent law).
5   *Id.* at 547-548.
6   *Applying for Patents; Attorneys and agents*, UNITED STATES PATENT AND TRADEMARK OFFICE, https://www.uspto.gov/patents/basics/apply.
7   *Id.*

inventions, aligning them with legal requirements to secure intellectual property rights.[8] The role and importance of patent attorneys is crucial for anyone involved in the legal or technological fields. A patent attorney is not just a lawyer, the patent attorney is often the link between innovation and legal protection, playing a pivotal role in the advancement of technology and the economy.

The patent attorney specialization contrasts sharply with other legal roles. Where a corporate lawyer may focus on business law and transactions, a patent attorney delves into the technical world of inventions.[9] The job is not just about understanding the law; it is about translating complex technical ideas into legally sound and protected patents.

One notable characteristic of patent attorneys is their demographic skew towards a more seasoned age compared to their non-patent counterparts. This isn't a random occurrence. In fact, it's rooted in the prerequisites set by the United States Patent and Trademark Office (USPTO).[10] To obtain a registration number—a ticket into the world of patent law—a prospective attorney must have a background in science or engineering.[11] As a result, many patent attorneys embark on this legal journey after a previous career, often in a technical field. This career trajectory adds a layer of depth and experience to their legal practice, making them not just attorneys but also experts in technological domains.

Becoming a patent attorney is a journey that requires a unique

---

8   *Id.*

9   Adam Hayes, *Patent Attorney: Who They are, What They do,* Investopedia (Dec. 5, 2022), https://www.investopedia.com/terms/p/patent-attorney.asp#:~:text=Patent%20attorneys%20are%20experts%20in,licensing%2C%20and%20re%2Dexamination.

10 *Applying for Patents; Attorneys and agents,* United States Patent And Trademark Office, https://www.uspto.gov/patents/basics/apply.

11 *Applying for Patents; Attorneys and agents,* United States Patent And Trademark Office, https://www.uspto.gov/patents/basics/apply; *See also* Adam Hayes, *Patent Attorney: Who They are, What They do,* INVESTOPEDIA (Dec. 5, 2022), https://www.investopedia.com/terms/p/patent-attorney.asp#:~:text=Patent%20attorneys%20are%20experts%20in,licensing%2C%20and%20re%2Dexamination.

blend of education and skills. Prospective patent attorneys must not only have a comprehensive understanding of the law, particularly patent law, but also possess a solid foundation in science or engineering.[12] This dual expertise is rare and highly valued.

The journey often begins with an undergraduate degree in a technical field, such as engineering or biology, followed by law school. However, the learning does not stop there. Patent attorneys must continually stay abreast of both legal developments and technological advancements, making the career a lifelong learning experience.[13]

What does the Patent Attorney Do?

A patent attorney plays a multifaceted role within the realm of intellectual property law, encompassing a wide range of functions that are critical to the protection and management of patents. At the core of these functions are two key areas: patent prosecution work and opinion work. Each of these areas requires a deep understanding of both legal principles and technical details, making the patent attorney's role both challenging and indispensable.

Patent prosecution, unlike what the term might suggest, does not involve litigation or legal disputes in the courtroom. Instead, it refers to the process of writing and filing a patent application and then guiding it through the Patent Office until a decision is made.[14] This is a meticulous and complex task, requiring not only a deep understanding of patent law but also a solid grasp of the technical subject matter of the invention, as the goal of patent prosecution is not just to obtain a patent, but to secure the broadest possible protection for the invention, ensuring a strong legal standing against potential infringements.

---

12 *Id.*
13 *Id.*
14 *Patent process overview*, UNITED STATES PATENT AND TRADEMARK OFFICE, https://www.uspto.gov/patents/basics/patent-process-overview.

Opinion work, on the other hand, involves providing expert legal opinions on critical aspects of patent law, such as patent validity and infringement. These opinions are vital for clients looking to understand the legal landscape of their inventions or products. Patent validity opinions in-volve a detailed analysis of a patent or a patent application to assess its strength and enforceability. This includes examining the invention's novelty, non-obviousness, and the adequacy of its disclosure. Such opinions are crucial for clients considering patent enforcement actions, licensing agreements, or investments in patented technology, as they provide a clear understanding of the patent's legal robustness. As it is said in the business, one can always get a patent; whether the patent is valid or even useful is another question. Interestingly, patents that have been granted but are likely invalid are often referred to as "zombie patents," and they are as scary as they sound.

Patent infringement opinions focus on whether a particular product or process infringes upon the claims of an existing patent. This involves a comparative analysis of the accused product and the patent claims to determine the likelihood of infringement. These opinions are essential for clients looking to launch new products, as they help navigate the risk of potential litigation and inform strategic decisions about product design and development. These opinions can also help a client decide whether to assert their patent rights against a product found to infringe one of their patents.[15]

Patent attorneys, therefore, stand at a unique intersection of law and technology. They must be able to understand the intricate details of an invention, often in cutting-edge fields like biotechnology, computer science, or mechanical engineering, and then translate these technical details into a legal format that aligns with the stringent

---

15   *Id.*

requirements of patent law.

In addition to the core functions of patent prosecution work and opinion work, patent attorneys also engage in the crucial role of broader patent strategy and portfolio management of their clients.[16] They advise on what inventions to patent, considering both the legal viability and the strategic value of the patents in the context of the client's business objectives.[17] In managing a patent portfolio, patent attorneys assess the strength and scope of existing patents, identify gaps in protection, and advise on potential expansions or improvements. This role involves a strategic vision, aligning the patent portfolio with the business's long-term goals and competitive landscape.[18] Indeed, the landscape of patent practice is rife with examples where an invention might initially seem valuable but may not hold as much value from a patent perspective. This discrepancy often arises from a misalignment between the inherent characteristics of the invention and the strategic objectives or market realities of the client's business.

One classic example involves technological advancements that are too far ahead of their time. While these inventions may represent significant scientific breakthroughs, their market applicability might be limited due to current technological limitations or consumer readiness. Patenting such innovations might not yield the expected competitive advantage or ROI, as the market for these technologies may not develop within the lifespan of the patent.

Another scenario is when an invention represents a marginal improvement over existing solutions. These incremental advancements

---

16   *What is Involved in Patent Portfolio Management*, SUPER LAWYERS (May 4, 2023), https://www.superlawyers.com/resources/patents/georgia/what-is-involved-in-patent-portfolio-management/.

17   *Id., See also* Camila Kiyomi Conegundes De Jesus and Mario Sergio Salerno, *Patent portfolio management: literature review and a proposed model* (May 9, 2018), https://www.tandfonline.com/doi/full/10.1080/13543776.2018.1472238?scroll=top&needAccess=true.

18   *What is Involved in Patent Portfolio Management*, SUPER LAWYERS (May 4, 2023), https://www.superlawyers.com/resources/patents/georgia/what-is-involved-in-patent-portfolio-management/.

might technically qualify for a patent, but their strategic value could be minimal. Competitors can easily design around these patents without infringing, or the market might not value the slight improvements enough to justify the costs of obtaining and enforcing the patent.

Similarly, inventions that are highly niche or specialized to the extent that they only serve a very small market segment might not offer substantial strategic value from a patent perspective. While securing a patent might grant exclusivity, the commercial payoff might not align with the investment if the target market is too limited.

Moreover, the evolving legal and regulatory landscape can render certain types of inventions less valuable from a patenting perspective. For instance, changes in patent law regarding software and business method patents have made it more challenging to obtain broad, enforceable patents in these areas. An invention in these domains might be innovative and useful but could face significant hurdles in securing patent protection that is both broad enough to be strategically valuable and strong enough to withstand legal challenges.

Patent attorneys, through their expertise, help navigate these complexities, advising clients on not just the legal viability but also the strategic foresight necessary to discern which inventions truly merit the investment in patent protection. This nuanced understanding ensures that resources are allocated to securing patents that align with and advance the client's business objectives, thereby optimizing the overall value of their IP portfolio.

To give a specific example, take a tech company that developed a cutting-edge software algorithm that significantly improved the efficiency of data processing. The invention seemed valuable because it offered a competitive edge in the market. However, upon closer examination, several factors showed the invention to be less valuable from a patent perspective.

Firstly, the algorithm's functionality was too abstract, which likely means the algorithm would not be patentable in many jurisdictions, including the United States. Secondly, the market was already saturated with similar solutions, even if they were not identical. In fact, prior art searches revealed that the algorithm, while novel in its specifics, operated in a manner closely related to then existing technologies. This narrowed the scope of potential patent claims so much that any resulting patent would have offered little to no competitive advantage or defense against infringement by others. Lastly, the rapidly evolving nature of the technology in the particular field meant that by the time a patent is granted, the market would likely have moved on to newer solutions, rendering the patent irrelevant. In this case, the client was advised to consider alternative strategies for protecting their product, such as maintaining the algorithm as a trade secret or even a copyright, rather than go through the expensive process of attempting to obtain a patent.

International Patent Law and Global Strategies

In today's global economy, the role of a patent attorney often extends beyond domestic borders. They must have a working knowledge of international patent systems and treaties, such as the Patent Cooperation Treaty (PCT).[19] Advising clients on international patent strategies involves understanding the nuances of patent law in different jurisdictions and coordinating patent filings to maximize global protection.[20]

How does the Patent Attorney Become a Patent Attorney?

---

19 *PCT - The International Patent System*, WIPO, https://www.wipo.int/pct/en/; *See also Summary of the Patent Cooperation Treaty* (PCT) (1970), WIPO, https://www.wipo.int/treaties/en/registration/pct/summary_pct.html.

20 *International Laws Involving Patents*, JUSTIA, https://www.justia.com/intellectual-property/patents/international-patent-protection/.

The path to becoming a patent attorney is rigorous and unique. Beyond a law degree, a patent attorney typically holds an undergraduate (and often advanced) degree in a scientific or technical field.[21] This dual expertise is a prerequisite to understanding the inventions they deal with and the complexities of patent law.[22]

Unlike many legal professionals who embark directly on their law careers after completing their education, patent attorneys often enter the field at a later stage. This unique trajectory is influenced by the prerequisite of having a technical or scientific background. As a result, the average age of patent attorneys tends to be higher than that of their counterparts in other legal specializations.[23]

Many patent attorneys begin their professional journey in technical roles, such as engineers, scientists, or researchers. This experience not only provides them with the necessary technical expertise but also offers a real-world perspective on innovation and its challenges.[24] The decision to transition to law typically comes after several years of working in these technical fields, leading to a demographic profile where patent attorneys are often in their mid-30s or older when they start practicing patent law.

The United States Patent and Trademark Office (USPTO) mandates that individuals must possess a certain level of technical expertise to be eligible to practice as patent attorneys. This requirement ensures that patent attorneys are well-equipped to understand and articulate complex scientific and technological concepts, a fundamental aspect of their role. [25]

---

21   *How to Become a Patent Lawyer: A Comprehensive Overview*, CLIO, https://www.clio.com/resources/how-to-become-a-lawyer/patent-lawyer/.

22   *Id.*

23   Julia DiPrete, *The Unusual Career Path of a Patent Attorney*, VAULT (Mar. 10, 2023), https://vault.com/blogs/vaults-law-blog-legal-careers-and-industry-news/the-unusual-career-path-of-a-patent-attorney.

24   *Id.*

25   *Becoming a Patent Practitioner,* UNITED STATES PATENT AND TRADEMARK OFFICE, https://www.uspto.gov/learning-and-resources/patent-and-trademark-practitioners/becoming-patent-practitioner.

This technical experience is typically verified through academic qualifications in fields such as engineering, physics, chemistry, biology, or computer science. In some cases, equivalent practical experience in a technical field can also fulfill this requirement. This prerequisite sets patent attorneys apart from other legal professionals, who may not need such specialized technical training.[26]

The educational backgrounds of patent attorneys are as diverse as the fields of science and technology itself. While many hold undergraduate and even graduate degrees in traditional STEM fields, some come from more specialized or emerging disciplines. This diversity reflects the wide range of inventions and technological advancements that patent attorneys work with.

For instance, a patent attorney with a background in biomedical engineering might specialize in patents related to medical devices, while someone with a degree in computer science might focus on software or internet technologies. This variety in educational backgrounds contributes to the richness of the patent law field, allowing for a deep and nuanced understanding of a broad spectrum of inventions.

The transition from a technical career to a legal one is a significant shift that requires not only a change in professional focus but also a substantial amount of additional education and training. For many patent attorneys, this transition is driven by a desire to combine their love for technology with the intellectual challenge of law.

Their previous careers often provide them with valuable insights into the practical aspects of technological innovation, including the challenges of research and development, the process of bringing new technologies to market, and the competitive dynamics of the tech industry. This real-world experience can be incredibly beneficial in

---

26   *Id.*

their legal practice, allowing them to offer more practical and informed advice to their clients. [27]

Continuous learning is a hallmark of successful patent attorneys, as given the rapidly evolving nature of both technology and law, patent attorneys must be committed to lifelong learning. They must stay updated on the latest legal precedents, changes in patent laws, and technological advancements. [28]. This commitment to ongoing education ensures they remain effective advocates for their clients in a rapidly evolving landscape.[29] This requirement for ongoing education and professional development is a distinctive aspect of a career in patent law. It demands a high level of intellectual curiosity and a commitment to staying informed about the latest legal precedents, technological breakthroughs, and industry trends. [30]

Effective patent attorneys build strong relationships with inventors and business stakeholders. They must be able to communicate complex legal and technical concepts in a clear and understandable manner, bridging the gap between inventors' technical expertise and the legal requirements of patent law.[31] This collaboration often involves educating inventors on the patent process and working closely with them to ensure that the patent applications accurately and fully describe their inventions. It also involves understanding the business context to ensure that the patent strategy aligns with the business objectives.

---

27 *The Crucial Role of Technical Expertise in Patent Services*, LINKEDIN (Feb. 2, 2024), https://www.linkedin.com/pulse/crucial-role-technical-expertise-patent-services-lawians-llp-8i96f/?trk=public_post_main-feed-card_reshare_feed-article-content.

28 *How to Become a Patent Lawyer: A Comprehensive Overview*, CLIO, https://www.clio.com/resources/how-to-become-a-lawyer/patent-lawyer/.

29 *Id.*

30 *Id.*

31 *Id.*

How does the Patent Attorney Think?

The demographic profile of patent attorneys reflects the unique intersection at which they operate – between law and technology. It's a field that attracts individuals who are not only passionate about science and technology but are also drawn to the intellectual rigor and challenges of the legal profession.

This blend of interests and skills shapes the patent law community, making it a dynamic and diverse group of professionals. From younger attorneys who have quickly transitioned from a technical degree to law, to seasoned professionals who bring years of industry experience, the range of backgrounds enriches the field and enhances the collective expertise of patent attorneys.

An Analytical Mind

At the core of a patent attorney's skill set is an intensely analytical mind. This trait is not merely a preference but a necessity in the field of patent law. The nature of the work requires a meticulous examination of both legal principles and technical details. Patent attorneys must analyze complex technical information and distill it into clear, concise, and legally sound patent claims.[32]

Their analytical abilities extend beyond understanding the invention itself; they must also anticipate potential legal challenges, understand the nuances of patent law, and foresee how changes in law and technology might impact the patents they draft. This level of analysis requires a keen attention to detail and the ability to think several steps ahead. [33]

Patent attorneys are adept at categorizing information and

---

32   *What Do Patent Attorneys Do: Everything You Need to Know* (Feb. 1, 2023), https://www.upcounsel.com/what-do-patent-attorneys-do.

33   *Id.*

recognizing patterns. This skill is crucial when reviewing patent applications, where they need to identify similarities and differences with existing patents. It's a skill that helps them navigate the vast landscape of patent law, where understanding how different cases and rulings relate to each other is key to forming effective legal strategies.[34]

Pattern recognition also plays a critical role in assessing the potential for patent infringement or in determining the novelty of an invention. By comparing and contrasting an invention with prior art, patent attorneys can more accurately gauge the likelihood of securing patent protection and advise their clients accordingly.

Logical reasoning is a fundamental aspect of a patent attorney's approach to problem-solving. They approach legal challenges methodically, breaking down complex issues into more manageable components. This logical process helps them to construct clear and persuasive arguments, whether in writing patent applications, responding to patent office actions, or advising clients on patent strategy. [35]

Problem-Solving Mind

Problem-solving for patent attorneys often involves finding creative legal solutions to protect an invention, considering all possible angles to strengthen a patent's defensibility. Their ability to think creatively within the confines of legal and technical frameworks is a testament to their problem-solving skills. [36] In some cases, the problem-solving skills of a patent attorneys extends beyond traditional legal maneuvers into the realm of creative strategy. For example, it is known that some

---

34   *Id.*

35   Andrea Brewster, *Essential Skills to become a successful Patent Attorney,* IP CAREERS, https://www.ipcareers.co.uk/profession-overview/essential-skills-for-patent-attorneys/#:~:text=Patent%20attorneys%20have%20to%20analyse,evidence%2C%20comprehensive%20in%20your%20approach.

36   *What Do Patent Attorneys Do: Everything You Need to Know,* UPCOUNSEL (Feb. 1, 2023), https://www.upcounsel.com/what-do-patent-attorneys-do.

patent attorneys may encourage their clients to attend interviews with patent examiners. This approach leverages a more personal element in the patent prosecution process. By bringing inventors into the conversation, patent attorneys humanize the invention beyond the pages of the application. Examiners, faced with the person whose ingenuity and hard work are encapsulated in the patent documents, may become more amenable to understanding the invention's nuances and significance. This interaction can break down barriers, making the examiner more receptive to the attorney's arguments and more inclined to consider allowances over rejections. In one notable instance, a patent attorney faced significant challenges with a patent examiner who was steadfast in their objections to a client's application. Recognizing the impasse, the attorney arranged for the inventor to attend a meeting with the examiner. The inventor's passion and direct explanation of the invention's development, its challenges, and its potential impact shifted the dynamics of the discussion. The examiner, seeing the invention through the inventor's eyes, reconsidered the application's merits, leading to a more favorable outcome.

A Precise and Adaptable Mind

The precision required in patent law cannot be overstated. A single word in a patent claim can be the difference between broad protection for an invention and a loophole that leaves it vulnerable. Patent attorneys possess an extraordinary attention to detail, necessary for crafting patent claims and legal arguments.[37]

This precision extends to all aspects of their work, from ensuring compliance with procedural requirements to maintaining the accuracy of technical descriptions. It's a characteristic that ensures the quality

---

37   *Id.*

and reliability of their work, which is crucial in the high-stakes world of intellectual property.

The field of technology is in constant flux, with new inventions and innovations emerging at a rapid pace. Patent attorneys must not only keep pace with these changes but also understand them deeply enough to provide effective legal counsel. [38]

This adaptability is a defining characteristic of successful patent attorneys. They are lifelong learners, continually updating their technical knowledge and staying abreast of the latest developments in both technology and patent law.

A Collaborative Mind

While technical and legal expertise are paramount, the role of a patent attorney also involves significant client interaction. They must be able to communicate complex legal and technical concepts in a way that clients can understand. This requires strong interpersonal skills and the ability to build trust and rapport with clients.

Patent attorneys often work closely with inventors, understanding their goals and concerns, and providing guidance throughout the patent process. This client-focused approach is essential for building long-term relationships and ensuring that the legal strategies align with the clients' broader business objectives. [39]

---

38   *Inventors 101: What Exactly is a Patent Attorney?* (Oct. 14, 2024), https://patentlawyer.io/what-is-patent-attorney/#:~:text=Since%20the%20field%20of%20patent,the%20duration%20of%20their%20careers.

39   Andrea Brewster, *Essential Skills to become a successful Patent Attorney,* IP CAREERS, https://www.ipcareers.co.uk/profession-overview/essential-skills-for-patent-attorneys/#:~:text=Patent%20attorneys%20have%20to%20analyse,evidence%2C%20comprehensive%20in%20your%20approach.

2

Here Goes the Patent Attorney

The role of a patent attorney is not just limited to a legal advisor but includes being a guardian of intellectual creativity, within the labyrinth of modern innovation, where the change in technology is happening all too fast. With the world now standing on the edge entering a new paradigm shift—marked by the relentless march of AI—the expertise and foresight of patent attorneys have never been more critical, even as their roles are fundamentally transformed. This chapter relates their professional biographies and reveals some of the detailed—often unnoticed—work that lies behind protection from the bastions of human ingenuity.

The domain of patent law is like no other, representing a very conjoined confine of science, technology, and jurisprudence that insists practitioners not only understand the gravitas and complexity associated with cutting-edge innovations but also learn to navigate the labyrinthine mazes of legal statutes and precedents. In short, the life of a patent attorney is wholly a part and parcel of their multi-disciplined role that brings together the analytical powers of a scientist, the strategic thinking of a chess master, and the argumentative fervor of a litigator. This chapter will focus on four core activities that a patent attorney typically performs: Patent Search, Patent Drafting, Patent Prosecution, and Opinion Work.

Patent Search

Patent Search is actually an intensive search of the existing patents and scientific documents, somewhat like the archaeologist's search, with the aim to find any prior arts that may reflect on the novelty of a new invention. This step is crucial for the potential success of a patent application and for paving the way for future innovations.

Patent Drafting

The drafting of a patent application is an art in itself. It requires a precise and detailed description of the invention, along with claims that define the scope of the patent protection being sought.[40] These claims must be carefully crafted to ensure they are broad enough to provide substantial protection, yet specific enough to satisfy the requirements of the patent office. This task often involves an intricate blend of legal acumen and strategic foresight, where understanding a client's business objectives and the broader competitive landscape is just as crucial as the legal process itself. When patent attorneys embark on drafting a patent, they're not merely navigating the legalities; they're embedding within each claim a deep strategic vision tailored to the client's specific business goals. For instance, a client might prioritize a defensive strategy, seeking patents to fortify their IP portfolio against potential litigation or to deter competitors from encroaching on their market space. This "poisoning the well" approach ensures that they remain unassailable, safeguarding their innovations from aggressive legal challenges. Conversely, some clients adopt an offensive stance, using their patents as a spearhead to secure a dominant position in their industry, potentially challenging competitors and carving out significant market share. Budget considerations also play a pivotal role, influencing the breadth

---

40   Emmanuel E. Jelsch, *Topic 9: Claim Drafting Techniques*, WIPO, https://www.wipo.int/edocs/
mdocs/aspac/en/wipo_ip_phl_16/wipo_ip_phl_16_t9.pdf.

and depth of the patent application process to align with financial constraints while still achieving the desired protective coverage. Each of these strategies—defensive, offensive, or budget-conscious—requires the patent attorney to anticipate various scenarios, from competitor reactions to patent office objections, crafting claims that not only withstand scrutiny but also align seamlessly with the client's overarching business vision.

Patent Prosecution

Patent Prosecution, as we are using herein, involves interacting with the patent office, moving the application for a patent towards issuance through persuasive arguments, and refining the application to clearly bring forth the novelty and usefulness of the invention. For example, once a patent application is filed, the patent attorney's role shifts to navigating the complex procedures of the Patent Office. This includes responding to actions and objections raised by patent examiners, who scrutinize applications for compliance with patent laws and regulations.[41] Patent attorneys engage in a nuanced dialogue with patent examiners, often negotiating the scope of the patent claims. This patent prosecution process can involve substantial back-and-forth, requiring the attorney to be adept at both legal argumentation and technical explanation.

Opinion Work

Opinion work is a cornerstone of a patent attorney's duties, offering specialized legal opinions that address the infringement and validity of patents. This service is indispensable for guiding businesses through the complex web of intellectual property, allowing them to

---

41   *Id.*

identify both the risks and opportunities their innovations may face in the marketplace. Central to opinion work is the execution of Freedom to Operate (FTO) analyses, infringement analyses, and patent validity analyses, each serving a distinct purpose in the intellectual property strategy of a business.

An FTO analysis is crucial for businesses aiming to launch a new product, as it assesses the potential risk of infringing existing patents, ensuring that the path to commercialization is clear of legal hurdles. Similarly, infringement analysis offers a detailed examination of whether a competitor's product may be infringing on the client's patents, a vital step for protecting intellectual property rights and deciding on enforcement actions. Lastly, patent validity analysis evaluates the strength and enforceability of a patent, which is crucial for understanding its likelihood to withstand challenges and its value in offensive or defensive strategies.

By weaving together these critical assessments, opinion work provides businesses with the strategic advice needed to navigate the minefield of intellectual property successfully. It ensures that clients can confidently commercialize their ideas, armed with a comprehensive understanding of the legal landscape and their position within it. Through this detailed approach, patent attorneys play an essential role in helping businesses establish a secure and competitive stance in the market, leveraging the full power of their innovations.

A Week in the Life of a Patent Attorney

What better way to shine a light on the battles of innovation than offering a view into the life of a patent attorney. As we delve into a week in the life of a patent attorney, we find ourselves going behind the lines into the battlefields of invention: where ideas are born and fought over. This exercise highlights the indispensable role that patent attorneys play in the progress of technology but at the same time sets one thinking on the future of the patent attorney with the advent of AI.

Day One - Patent Search

The first day of our patent attorney's week kicks off with a crucial task: diving into a patent search. Far from being just another item on the to-do list, this involves a deep dive into existing patents and academic works to make sure the invention they're championing hasn't already been claimed by someone else. It's like setting out on a treasure hunt, scouring the vast landscape of innovation to see if the unique idea your inventor has come up with has already been found and claimed by another pioneer in the field.

As daylight breaks and the coffee starts brewing, the attorney gets down to business, examining the invention with a keen eye. They're not just skimming the surface; they're looking at the invention inside and out, focusing on what makes it tick. With this understanding, they map out a search strategy, picking out databases, keywords, and classifications with the precision of a tailor fitting a suit, ensuring it perfectly matches the invention's unique profile.

When midday rolls around, armed with a carefully laid out plan, the attorney sets off on their search journey. Far from being a task that can be approached passively, the patent search demands engagement and active participation. Our attorney does not just skim but actually delves deep into databases filled with patents, scientific papers, etc. In doing so, our attorney uses a set of keywords and classifications, previously thought out and defined. It's similar, you might say, to what an archaeologist does during an excavation. Every paper, every patent, turns into a potential hint, a piece of the puzzle in grasping the broader picture of what's already out there. And it's up to our attorney to figure out how each piece fits in relation to the invention at hand.

Sometimes, the complexity of the invention means calling in the cavalry—an external search firm known for their skill in navigating the tricky terrain of patent searches. The attorney lays out a detailed plan for these experts, clearly marking the intellectual gems they're hunting for. It's not just about passing the baton; it's about teaming up with the best of the best to ensure the search is as thorough and effective as possible.

The search team gets to work, sifting through mountains of documents with the focus of detectives on the hunt for hidden clues. Their goal? To find any prior art that might stake a claim before their inventor does.

As the afternoon wanes, our attorney turns detective, poring over the search results with a fine-toothed comb. It's like piecing together a jigsaw puzzle without the picture on the box, a challenging but thrilling task. Each piece of prior art found is carefully documented, its relevance and impact on the inventor's story assessed.

As the day winds down, it's time to pull together everything that's been discovered into a comprehensive report. This isn't just a recap of the day's work; it's a strategic blueprint for what comes next. It sets the stage for a deep dive discussion with the inventor, where insights are shared, and future tactics are planned out.

In the quiet moments at day's end, the attorney reflects on the day's journey. It was all about laying down a solid foundation to ensure a smooth and clear path for the patenting process ahead. This first day is just the start of what promises to be an exciting adventure through the drafting and prosecution stages, setting a thoughtful and energetic pace for the days to follow.

Days Two and Three - Patent Drafting

Days Two and Three bring the intricate dance of patent drafting. In this domain, the fine line between precision and creativity is navigated with expertise and flair.

Day Two- Patent Drafting

Day Two dawns, and it's time for 'The Deep Dive'. Think of our attorney, not just equipped but fully immersed in a sea of technical detail, ranging from voluminous reports to the simplicity of an idea captured on a napkin. The task at hand is no small feat; it's about distilling vast oceans of information into the pure essence of the invention. It's akin to a treasure hunt where the treasure is the core innovation hidden within mountains of data or in the sparse lines of a preliminary idea. This phase is not just about sifting through information; it's a deep dive into consultation with technical wizards and further research to grasp the invention in its entirety. Imagine the detective work, the technical deep dives, all aimed at capturing the innovation's true breadth and depth.

By the time the sun reaches its zenith, our attorney is deep in the trenches of drafting patent claims. This task transcends mere understanding; it requires a visionary approach, anticipating the trajectories of future technologies. The claims crafted are not just shields but also swords, designed to protect the invention in its current state and as it evolves into future forms. Each word is meticulously chosen, akin to laying bricks for a fortress, where each brick is a word, each layer a sentence, strategically placed for maximum protection.

As the day unfolds into the afternoon, a different kind of craftsmanship comes into play – storytelling. Beyond the mechanical and the technical, our attorney embarks on narrating the saga of the invention. This narrative weaves through the development journey, spotlighting challenges and epiphanies. It's a narrative that breathes life into the patent, transforming it from a document of technical jargon into a testament of human ingenuity and perseverance. This story is for everyone - from those who scrutinize patents in the offices to the curious minds in the future who seek to understand the genesis of an innovation.

As twilight beckons, a moment of pause ensues. It's a time for reflection, not just on the minutiae but on the grand canvas. Is the essence of the invention captured in its entirety? Does the draft not only narrate but also strategize for the invention's future trajectory? This reflective process is a crucial checkpoint, ensuring the application's strategic alignment with its technical precision.

Day Three - Patent Drafting Continuation

With the break of Day Three, the attorney revisits the draft with a renewed vision, ready to refine and expand. This day is about adding layers, weaving in examples of the invention's applications, and exploring alternative embodiments to cast a wider net of protection. It's about bolstering the draft, transforming it into a bastion of innovation, impervious to future challenges.

The collaborative spirit intensifies by midday, turning the process into a confluence of minds. The attorney and the inventor delve deeper, exploring the invention's nuances and any emergent innovations. This collaborative endeavor extends to peers, whose fresh perspectives and critical insights add another layer of depth, ensuring the application's integrity and coherence.

In the afternoon, the focus shifts to polishing, where every detail is magnified, every format scrutinized, every drawing clarified. It's a labor of meticulous attention, ensuring that the application not only meets but exceeds the formal requirements, presenting the invention in the best possible light.

As Day Three draws to a close, the gaze turns towards the horizon, preparing for the journey ahead. It's about strategizing for the submission, anticipating the patent office's challenges, and readying responses. The drafting odyssey has prepared the attorney not just for submission but for navigating the examination process with strategic foresight.

Reflecting on this journey, our attorney stands at the intersection of art and science, advocate and strategist. It's a testament to the nuanced art of patent drafting, a blend of advocacy, strategy, and storytelling, navigating the intricate legal landscapes to safeguard innovation. With the draft now honed to perfection, the path forward is illuminated, and our attorney is poised, ready to face the forthcoming adventures with confidence and expertise.

Day Four- Patent Prosecution

Day Four welcomes us to a whole new battlefield in the patent world: patent prosecution. This isn't about legal battles in courtrooms but rather the strategic back-and-forth with the patent office. It's a day where our attorney dons the hat of a negotiator, a strategist, and sometimes, a bit of a soothsayer, predicting how best to navigate the intricate dance of getting a patent across the finish line.

The day kicks off with a review of where each application stands in the prosecution process. Our attorney is lining up their cases like chess pieces, strategizing moves for each. They're diving into the latest communications from the patent office—these could be Notices of Allowance (the golden ticket), Office Actions (a mix of minor hiccups and major roadblocks), or Requests for Information. Each communication demands a tailored response, and our attorney is mapping out their plan of attack.

By midday, we're deep in the trenches of responding to Office

Actions. These documents from the patent office can range from straightforward requests for clarification to complex rejections based on prior art or patentability issues. Our attorney is part analyst, part wordsmith here, dissecting the patent office's concerns and crafting responses that advocate for the invention's novelty and non-obviousness. They're pulling from case law, tweaking claims, and sometimes proposing amendments to navigate around the cited prior art. It's meticulous work, requiring a keen understanding of both the invention and the nuances of patent law.

Afternoons often bring consultations with inventors or the R&D team. These sessions are crucial, especially when complex technical issues are at stake. Our attorney is translating the legalese of the Office Actions into actionable insights for the inventors, gathering additional arguments, or clarifying technical points that could strengthen the response. It's a collaborative effort, with the goal of ensuring that the revised application or response fully captures the invention's essence and overcomes the examiner's concerns.

As the afternoon wanes, it's time for forward planning. Our attorney is not just responding to current Office Actions but also anticipating the next steps. This involves reviewing upcoming deadlines, preparing for potential interviews with patent examiners, and strategizing about appeal options if necessary. They're also checking in with clients, updating them on the status of their applications, and setting expectations for the road ahead.

Day Four ends with a moment of reflection. Patent prosecution can be a rollercoaster, with its ups and downs dictated by the back-and-forth with the patent office. Our attorney takes stock of the day's accomplishments, the responses crafted, the consultations conducted, and the plans set for the next steps. There's satisfaction in navigating these challenges, in finding the right words and arguments that move an invention closer to being granted a patent.

With the prosecution process well underway for several applications, our attorney looks ahead to the next challenges and opportunities. The work of patent prosecution is a blend of legal expertise, technical understanding, and strategic foresight. And as Day Four comes to a close, there's a keen anticipation for what the next day will bring, ready to tackle whatever the patent office might have in store.

Days Five through Seven - Opinion Work

Days Five through Seven unfold as a pivotal juncture in our narrative, marking a transition from the drafting desks to the dynamic arena of providing legal opinion. On these days, our attorney will don the hat of a seasoned navigator to guide clients through the minefield of existing patents and potential legal battles. Our patent attorney is part detective, part strategist, and all about protecting their clients' innovations and interests.

Day Five - the FTO

On Day Five, our patent attorney plunges into an FTO analysis, a critical first step for a new client poised at the brink of a product launch. Our attorney pores over patents and technical documents related to the features of the product, similar to a patent search but with a twist. The aim here is to ensure that the client's proposed product (or process) doesn't step on the toes of existing patents. It's like navigating a ship through a sea of legal icebergs, where each patent represents a potential collision course. Our attorney is mapping out a safe passage, identifying any potential risks and advising on how to steer clear or navigate through them.

This task is not for the faint-hearted. It demands a connoisseur's eye for detail and a strategist's mind to sift through countless patents, unraveling the intricate web of claims and counterclaims to secure a safe passage for the client's innovation. This process is reminiscent of a grandmaster playing a high-stakes game of chess, anticipating moves and countermoves, ensuring the client's product maneuvers clear of any legal entanglements.

The day ends with the generation of an FTO report, which includes an opinion by our patent attorney as to whether or not the client's proposed product infringes a patent. An opinion by our patent attorney that client's proposed product does not infringe a patent gives the client the freedom to continue commercialization with the opinion from an expert. Of course, the FTO is not infallible, as our patent attorney is still human. However, the FTO report, especially an opinion of non-infringement, can help the client avoid enhanced damages if he is found to infringe a patent after all, since the FTO report will show that the client did not act willfully or in bad faith. This is why the FTO report is so important and can be hugely beneficial to a client.

The day ends with the creation of a Freedom to Operate (FTO) report, which embodies our patent attorney's expert opinion on whether the client's proposed product potentially infringes any existing patents. This pivotal opinion, can empower the client to proceed with commercializing their innovation confidently, backed by expert legal advice affirming the absence of infringement, or can help the client make informed decisions to make changes to the product, or even discontinuing it altogether, when the FTO finds infringement.

It's important to recognize that while the FTO report is a critical tool, it is not infallible; after all, even the most seasoned patent attorney is human. However, an FTO report, particularly one that finds no infringement, plays a crucial role in mitigating the risk of enhanced damages in the event of a subsequent finding of infringement. This is because the report demonstrates that the client's actions were conducted in good faith, without willful disregard of patent laws. Thus, the FTO report emerges not just as a document, but as a strategic asset for the client, offering both guidance and a measure of protection in the complex landscape of intellectual property.

Day Six - Patent Infringement Analysis

By Day Six, the narrative intensifies as our patent attorney pivots to address a looming threat: a competitor's product that seems to tread too closely to our client's patented invention. This shift to infringement analysis marks a pivotal moment, blending the attorney's legal prowess with technical acumen to safeguard the client's innovations.

The day begins with a meticulous review of the client's patent portfolio, identifying the specific patents that the competitor's product might infringe. Our attorney, equipped with a detailed understanding of the patent claims and the technological landscape, prepares for a deep dive into the competitor's product. This preparation involves gathering all available information about the product, including technical specifications, marketing materials, and any publicly available demonstrations or teardowns.

By midday, our attorney is fully immersed in the forensic examination of the competitor's product. This analysis is not merely a side-by-side comparison; it's an investigative journey into the heart of the product's technology. Our attorney deconstructs every feature and function, mapping them against the claims of the client's patents to identify potential overlaps. Given the complexity of modern technology, this process often necessitates collaboration with technical experts who provide insights into the nuanced aspects of the product's design and operation.

With a comprehensive understanding of the technical details, the afternoon is dedicated to the legal assessment of the findings. Our attorney evaluates the strength of the potential infringement case, considering both the clear-cut aspects and the subtler, interpretive elements of patent law. This assessment weighs the likelihood of success in litigation against the broader strategic interests of the client, including the potential impact on their market position and ongoing innovation efforts.

Concluding that the competitor's product likely infringes upon our client's patent, our attorney moves to draft a cease-and-desist letter. This letter is not just a warning; it's a carefully crafted legal document that outlines the infringement findings, asserts the client's rights, and demands immediate cessation of the infringing activities. The goal is to resolve the issue amicably, if possible, by opening a channel for negotiation before escalating to litigation. This letter serves as a testament to our attorney's commitment to protecting the client's intellectual property, balancing assertiveness with an openness to dialogue.

As the day draws to a close, our attorney reflects on the intricate work of infringement analysis and the strategic decision to issue a cease-and-desist letter. This day highlights the attorney's role not just as a legal advisor but as a guardian of innovation, poised to defend the client's intellectual property rights against all encroachments. Looking ahead, our attorney prepares for potential responses to the cease-and-desist letter, strategizing next steps in case litigation becomes inevitable.

Day Seven- Patent Invalidity Analysis

Day Seven unfolds with our patent attorney at a pivotal juncture, shifting gears towards a deep analytical and strategic endeavor: drafting a patent validity opinion. This task, spurred by a client's resolve to challenge a competitor's patent, demands a thorough dissection of the patent in question, its origins, claims, and the intricate web of prior art surrounding it.

The day commences with our attorney setting the stage for this intricate analysis. This involves gathering all relevant documents related to the patent in question, including its prosecution history from the patent office, any related litigation documents, and the patent itself. The attorney begins a meticulous examination of the patent's lineage, tracing its claims back to the original application, amendments, and any office actions or responses. This historical context is crucial for understanding the patent's evolution and identifying any potential vulnerabilities.

By midday, the focus narrows to a detailed examination of the patent's claims and the surrounding prior art. Our attorney, equipped with a nuanced understanding of the technical field, pores over scientific journals, patents, and other publications to unearth prior art that may have been overlooked or undervalued during the patent's prosecution. This process is not just about identifying relevant prior art; it's about constructing a narrative that challenges the patent's originality and non-obviousness, key pillars of its validity.

The afternoon is dedicated to synthesizing the findings into a coherent strategy. Our attorney evaluates the strength of the potential challenge to the patent's validity, considering the uncovered prior art and any procedural missteps during the patent's prosecution. This assessment forms the backbone of the validity opinion, offering not just an analysis of the patent's weaknesses but also a strategic view on the likelihood of success in challenging the patent.

With a clear strategy in mind, our attorney begins drafting the patent validity opinion. This document is more than a report; it's a roadmap for navigating the complexities of patent litigation. It details the findings of the attorney's analysis, presents a strategic assessment of the patent's vulnerabilities, and advises on the best course of action. The opinion balances technical detail with strategic insight, offering clear guidance while highlighting the risks and opportunities of challenging the patent.

As Day Seven comes to a close, our attorney reflects on the strategic implications of their findings. The drafted patent validity opinion is a critical tool for the client, illuminating the path forward in challenging a rival's patent. It outlines not just the avenues for attack but also cautions against potential pitfalls. Looking ahead, our attorney prepares to discuss the findings with the client, ready to advise on the next steps in what could be a significant legal battle.

Week's End

As the week winds down, our patent attorney takes a well-earned pause, reflecting on a series of victories and accomplishments achieved on behalf of their clients. This period of respite brings into sharp relief the immense effort and extensive hours that went into securing each success. Throughout the week, the attorney has been a steadfast advocate for innovation, navigating the labyrinth of intellectual property law to protect and advance their clients' interests.

The week's journey was marked by long days filled with detailed analyses, strategic planning, and meticulous drafting—all aimed at ensuring the best possible outcomes for the clients. From conducting thorough patent searches to drafting robust patent applications, the attorney's expertise and diligence were pivotal. Each task, whether it was responding to office actions during patent prosecution or crafting nuanced legal opinions on potential infringements, required a significant investment of time and intellectual effort. The attorney's commitment to excellence was evident in their unwavering attention to detail and their relentless pursuit of every legal avenue available to serve their clients' needs.

However, this level of dedication, while admirable, underscored a broader challenge: the inherently time-consuming nature of traditional patent law practice. Each victory for a client, though rewarding, was a reminder of the countless hours spent in legal research, analysis, and documentation. The attorney's role as a beacon of guidance through the complex matrix of intellectual property was achieved through sustained effort, underscoring the demanding nature of the profession.

This backdrop of hard-won achievements, secured through relentless effort and dedication, sets the stage for a transformative possibility that we discuss in the coming chapters: the advent of AI in the realm of patent law. As we look ahead, we anticipate exploring how AI could revolutionize the way patent attorneys work. Imagine the same level of quality and thoroughness, achieved in a fraction of the time, with AI assisting in legal analysis, patent searches, and even drafting preliminary documents. The potential for AI to enhance efficiency without compromising on quality opens up exciting avenues for both patent attorneys and their clients, promising a future where innovation is protected and promoted more swiftly and effectively than ever before.

As our attorney looks forward to what lies ahead, the promise of AI integration in their practice offers a glimpse of a more efficient, dynamic approach to intellectual property law. The following chapters will delve into how AI stands to redefine the traditional workflows of patent attorneys, heralding a new era of legal practice where technology and human expertise converge to achieve exceptional outcomes in less time.

3

Here Comes AI

Human interest in AI dates back to the ancient Indians, Greeks, and Chinese. As Pamela McCorduch put it[42], AI began "with an ancient wish to forge the gods," which is further exemplified with the hubris of Paracelsus in the early 1500's when he said "We shall be like Gods. We shall duplicate God's greatest miracle - the creation of man." A familiar ancient mythological example of AI dates back to the 800's B.C. in Homer's *The Iliad*. It was referred to as the *Talos*, a winged bronze automaton forged by Hephaistos to protect Greece.

AI continued to pervade literature for centuries. Accounts ranged from benevolent, to playful, to mischievous, and even sinister. An example of a mischievous automaton from Jewish folklore is the "Golem," a creature supposedly created by a Rabbi using some form of magic. The Golem would carry out instructions (many from the Rabbi's wife) to a mischievously pedantic degree, which would ultimately result in its dismantling.

Other examples include "Moxon's monster," "Faust", and most notably Mary Shelley's "Frankenstein". The latter is a famous example of an intelligent, artificial agent ultimately becoming malevolent. The book is really quite interpretive, displaying some of Shelley's

---

42   Pamela McCorduck, Machines Who Think: A Personal Inquiry into the History and Prospects of Artificial Intelligence (1979).

interactions with the intellectual elite at the time[43].

At first glance, the novels "Dracula" by Braham Stoker and "Frankenstein" by Mary Shelley are very similar. However, in reality they differ drastically as to their insights on the human condition. In Shelley's novel, a scientist, Dr. Frankenstein, discovers a primordial element principal to life itself. Using his discovery, he stitches together a creature from cadavers. Leveraging electricity from a lightning strike, he is able to impart the creature with life.

Contrary to contemporary understanding, the monster was not named Frankenstein, but remained unnamed, likely to convey a detachment and even cruelty to this act of creation, evincing early sentiment about the topic. Themes of 'ungodliness' are prevalent throughout the work, and we often hear words like "vile," "abhorrent," etc. when referring to the creature, even from its own creator.

A little-known fact is the subtitle of "Frankenstein" was "The Modern Day Prometheus." In Greek mythology, Zeus ordered Prometheus to create humans. He also later brought them fire, for which he suffered an eternal punishment: endlessly pushing a rock up a hill and having his liver eaten by an eagle daily. His status as an immortal ensured that his liver would grow back, and he would repeat this punishment in perpetuity. The Prometheus reference is an allegory as to the desire to create life, or more abstractly, sentience or consciousness. Furthermore, the punishment Prometheus faced later could even foreshadow potential consequences of such an act[44].

Shelley's work was likely very much inspired by her circle of contemporaries at the time, one of which was Charles Babbage. Babbage is often accredited with devising the concept of the modern-day digital

---

43   Mary Shelly, Frankenstein (1993).
44   Olga Raggio, *The Myth of Prometheus: Its Survival and Metamorphoses up to the Eighteenth Century*, 21, J. of the Warburg and Courtauld Institutes, 44–62 (1958).

computer. He created plans for a mechanical prototype called the "Difference Engine," which was capable of calculating values of polynomials by implementing a mathematical technique known as "Finite Differences". This technique allowed him to avoid the complications of multiplication and division. Nevertheless, the plans for the Difference Engine were exceedingly complex, with over 20,000 parts involved, and Babbage never was able to complete the Difference Engine due to funding issues, a subject about which he remained bitter for the rest of his life. Unfortunately, though Babbage came from means, he died penniless in 1871. Nevertheless, some parts remain from his early manufacturing attempts to this day safely ensconced in the Museum of the History of Science, Oxford. His vision was finally realized in the early 1990's when researchers built the prototype to the specifications and manufacturing tolerances of his era. It is still able to make successful calculations to this day.

Mechanical Concepts

A more general version of the Difference Engine was devised by Babbage, called the "Analytical Engine". This concept was sufficiently more robust, and complicated, than the difference engine. It would allow a practitioner to interact with the device via holes in punched cards. Though it was not actually built until 2008, the robustness of the capabilities envisaged by Babbage, especially for the time, were truly astounding. The machine was capable of implementing control structures, branching, and looping, which constitute Turing Completeness (a concept we will revisit later). In other words, it was essentially a programmable computer[45].

---

45   Rebecca Bales, *The History of Charles Babbage's Analytical Engine, Ant the Birth of Computers*, HISTORY COMPUTER (Jul. 24, 2023), https://history-computer.com/charles-babbage-analytical-engine/.

If Babbage is to be considered the "Father of the Computer"[46], then Ada Lovelace was arguably its mother. She is often accredited as being the first computer programmer, helping to weave the mechanical algorithm which could perform complex computations such as the calculation of Bernoulli numbers.

Though neither Babbage nor Lovelace suggested that their machines could be 'thinking', they did acknowledge the possibility of components changing dynamically should the situation arise.

Electronic Prototypes

All of the above devices discussed thus far were mechanical in nature. Electronic computational devices did not follow until the 1940's. These were significant advances, and major steps toward breakthroughs that ultimately led to devices like the ones used today. Furthermore, though early AI implementations were still premature, we can observe a distinct focus on "thinking machines" in the documentation of contributing pioneers at this time.

The first electronic computational devices were primarily used to facilitate calculations for war efforts during World War 2. Konrad Zuse was a German civil engineer who developed one of the first of these machines, called the Z3, a practically Turing complete machine, which became operational in 1941. It was used to automate the extensive calculations of a Nazi Aviation research institute. The Nazi's funded the Z3 and many of Zuse's subsequent machines. Zuse filed many patents and is even accredited with the world's first programming language, Plankalkul. Although none of his work touched on any facet of artificial intelligence just yet, he did have "thinking machines" in mind. It should be noted that Zuse never became a member of the Nazi party,

---

46   Daniel Stephen Halacy, Charles Babbage, Father of the Computer (1970).

and later would concede that many of the scientists at the time had to make a Faustian bargain with the Nazis or be forced to discontinue their research (or worse)[47].

Other later computational machines included IBM's Mark 1, devised by Howard Aiken in 1944. The Mark 1 weighed over 10,000 lbs., was the size of a large room, and was powered by a 5-horsepower electric motor. It was used by the Navy Bureau of ships to perform calculations.

The "Colossus" computers were another series of computing machines devised by Tommy Flowers in the 1940's. The first working prototype was produced in 1943, with an improved version following a year later. By the end of the war there were ten functioning Colossus machines in use by British codebreakers to decipher encrypted teleprinter messages.

The ENIAC (Electronic Numerical Integrator and Computer), designed by John Mauchley and J. Presper Eckert was the first digital computer, a Turing complete machine that could solve a range of problems. It was designed to calculate firing tables for the US Army's Ballistic Research Laboratory. The contract for its construction was signed in 1943 and its completion was publicly announced in 1946[48].

A milestone in the development of computer science and artificial intelligence was the work of Alan Turing. A great deal of his research focused on the connection between thinking and computing machines. He was very much in favor of the notion of "thinking machines." Regarding such machines achieving human level cognition he once stated that it's "a short distance ahead" though he admitted it required much work. One of his great contributions was the notion of

---

47   Konrad Zuse, The Computer - My Life (2010).
48   Joel N. Shurkin, Engines of the Mind: The Evolution of the Computer from Mainframes to Microprocessors (1996).

the "Turing Machine" which he first proposed in 1936.

The idea of the Turing Machine gave birth to what we now know as "Computer Science". Turing built the groundwork to formalize concepts such as the "algorithm" and "computation". In his formulation, a "Turing Machine" is a device that manipulates symbols on a strip of tape according to a predefined set of rules. It can be shown that the logic of any computer algorithm (including Babbage's Analytical Engine) can ultimately be represented theoretically by a Turing Machine. This fact gives insight into the workings of the modern CPU. A Turing machine that can simulate any other Turing Machine is said to be a "Universal Turing Machine" (UTM). A system of rules is said to be "Turing Complete" if it can be used to simulate any single taped Turing Machine.

One popular example of a Turing Complete language is a "Lambda Calculus" which is a manner of expressing computation by a formal system that employs variable binding and substitution. The concept was first introduced by Alonzo Church in the 1930's in an effort to investigate the foundations of mathematics. Church would eventually serve as the doctoral advisor to Turing. The two would collaborate, combining their respective new ideas giving birth to the monumental "Church-Turing Thesis" which became a formal theory of computation that encapsulated the idea of formal method and procedure in mathematics and logic, and provided a precise definition for an "algorithm" in the computational sense. From this framework many formal boundaries and insights can be obtained pertaining to computation and complexity theory[49].

Believing in the potential of machines to approach "potentialities of human intelligence with suitable training," Turing argued all

---

49   ALONZO CHURCH, A SET OF POSTULATES FOR THE FOUNDATIONS OF LOGIC, 346-66 (1932).

contemporary objections regarding the notion. He noted that when with respect to human beings, it is implicitly understood that everyone thinks. This conjecture led to the formulation of the "Turing Test" in 1950, the first "litmus paper test" for General Artificial Intelligence at a human level. We will discuss this in detail later in this chapter.

Regrettably, Turing was a homosexual in an era of intense censure. His sexuality resulted in a criminal persecution in 1952. He accepted chemical castration by taking female hormones as an alternative to prison. Ostracization and threats led to his suicide by cyanide poisoning in 1954 just before his 42nd birthday. He was an enthusiast of amateur chemistry, often making concoctions from household chemicals. For this reason, some (including his mother) believe that his death was accidental, though it is generally deemed as a suicide.

The 20ᵗʰ Century

Though many of these great pioneers of mechanical automation flirted with the idea of "thinking machines," John Von Neumann advanced the field both computationally and theoretically. Von Neumann was a Hungarian mathematician of stunning intellectual caliber, who made many notable contributions to science and mathematics in fields ranging from set theory to geometry to quantum mechanics, and computer science. His design for a computer processor, the "Von Neumann Architecture," is still used in modern x86 CPU's[50].

Born to wealthy parents in Hungary, which was still the Austrio-Hungarian empire at the time, the precocious Von Neumann demonstrated mathematical prowess from a very early age. For example, he could divide two 8-digit numbers in his head by the age of 6. Although his father wanted him to study at the level of peers of his age, he did

---

50   HERMAN HEINE GOLDSTINE, THE COMPUTER FROM PASCAL TO VON NEUMANN (1993).

hire private tutors to foster the young Von Neumann's skills. His abilities stunned his tutors and even brought one to tears. By the age of 22 he earned his PhD in mathematics, accumulated numerous undergraduate degrees, and was well published.

In 1930, he was invited to Princeton to the Institute for Advanced study, home to the likes of Albert Einstein and Kurt Gödel among others. The Institute for Advanced study was meant to foster developments in highly theoretical and abstract disciplines, by providing an atmosphere where great thinkers could tinker and ponder unhindered by the demand for practicality from industry or government research institutions. Von Neumann's ideas for computational devices were often considered "too practical" for the institute, though it was there that he brought forth his creation. His digital computer was capable of executing a stored program. He taught at Princeton for the rest of his life, ultimately succumbing to cancer in 1954.

The neurological research of the time revealed the "all or nothing" nature of neural interactions. That is, in the presence of an electrical stimulus, the neuron either fired an electrical impulse, or it did not. Von Neumann was intrigued by this paradigm and made many explicit comparisons between his digital architectures and the human nervous system. He noted that the brain evinced both analogue and digital characteristics, though the mechanical computers of the time were limited to either analogue or digital, but not both. Until his death, he pined for a rigorous mathematical model of neural behavior, though he admitted to believing this was impossible. His research to this effect was published posthumously in his book "The Computer and the Brain" where he detailed a lot of the similarities and differences between the computers of the time and the brain and pioneered research into what we now know as Artificial Neural Networks[51].

Further research into ANNs was accompanied by some great computational developments. Norbert Wiener[52], fascinated by analogies of biological neurons and electronics, developed cybernetics which was first used to solve control and stability problems with electronic networks. Concurrently Claude Shannon was developing information theory[53], which used as a primary tool in writing "The Computational Theory of Intelligence."

Walter Pitts and Warren McColloch under Frank Rosenblatt were the first to model an idealized artificial version of biological neurons, the first ANN, a nascent version of the neural networks in use today[54]. Their research focused on emulating cognition by modeling systems of neurons. One of their students at MIT, Marvin Minsky would later become a great contributor to AI and computer science in general. It was the results of McColloch and Pitts that John Von Neumann would reference when he stated that "... anything that can be exhaustively and unambiguously described, anything that can be completely and unambiguously put into words is ipso facto realizable by a suitable finite neural network".

The invention of Pitts and McColluck was called a "Single Layer Perceptron." The design involves the application of a series of weights to an input vector, or series of data points. Using a process called "Supervised Learning" (discussed in more detail later), weights may be adjusted with respect to a training set, to achieve a desired outcome. Though implementations of the Perceptron exist to this day in code,

---

51 JOHN VON NEUMANN, THE COMPUTER AND THE BRAIN (3rd ed. 1958).
52 FLO CONWAY & JIM SIEGELMAN, DARK HERO OF THE INFORMATION AGE: IN SEARCH OF NORBERT WIENER - FATHER OF CYBERNETICS (2005).
53 CLAUDE ELWOOD SHANNON & WARREN WEAVER, THE MATHEMATICAL THEORY OF COMMUNICATION (1964).
54 Warren S. McCulloch & Walter Pitts, *A Logical Calculus of the Ideas Immanent in Nervous Activity*, 5, Bulletin of Mathematical Biology, 115-33 (1943).

remarkably Frank Rosenblatt built a physical representation of the concept called the "Mark 1 Perceptron Machine", designed for image recognition at Cornell Aeronautical Laboratory in 1957. It consisted of a 20-by-20 grid of photocells from which the input was fed to 512 weights in a "hidden layer". The final result was output via 8 "response units", a.k.a. the "output layer".

Although the first computational devices were made for wartime calculations, applications in gaming were not far behind. Arthur Samuel in 1952 at IBM build a checkers machine. In 1962 it would proceed to beat then checkers champion Robert Nealey. The checkers program functioned by evaluating its position on the board relative to the other pieces. It would then make a move which was considered to be optimal with respect to a "scoring function". It was designed to improve by employing what was essentially the first example of an "evolutionary algorithm", a subclass of AI, containing algorithms, many biologically inspired[55], such as Genetic Algorithms.

In 1958, John McCarthy originated the first incarnation of a programming language called LISP (short for LISt Processing). The language evolved into a family of languages and has made great strides since its inception. It is considered to be the second oldest contemporary programming language, second only to FORTRAN by one year. LISP was said to be very much inspired by Church's Lambda Calculus. LISP is used in AI programming and prototyping even today, and has several advantages. First, it facilitates prototyping, which proves utilitarian when attempting problems with which one has little knowledge. Second, it computes with symbols very well, alleviating the need for explicit numerical input[56]. Symbolic programming allows one to focus

---

55   DARIO FLOREANO & CLAUDIO MATTIUSSI, BIO-INSPIRED ARTIFICIAL INTELLIGENCE: THEORIES, METHODS, AND TECHNOLOGIES (2008).

56   PETER NORVIG, PARADIGMS OF ARTIFICIAL INTELLIGENCE PROGRAMMING: CASE STUDIES IN COMMON LISP (1st ed. (1992).

clearly on the problem at hand, and not have to worry about shuffling bits and data, in contrast to the drudgery of more "low level languages" such as C and C++.

A cornerstone in the development of AI, and its solidification as a field of study began with the Dartmouth conference in 1956[57]. It was originally envisioned by John McCarthy, but would later be formally proposed by McCarthy and other colleagues interested in the field including Marvin Minsky, Nathaniel Rochester, and Claude Shannon. The conference was essentially a two-month brainstorming session where ten invitees, including the originators of the conference would discuss topics such as intelligent machine automation, language interpretation and manipulation, neural networks and their ability to form concepts, the scale of calculations and their complexity, self-improvement, the ability to form abstractions of concepts, and finally, creativity.

The conference was the first of its kind. Many of the invitees were inspired and stimulated by the conference, compounded with the exciting developments in Computer Science in general at the time, such as Moore's law, which noted that the number of transistors in an integrated circuit (which is proportional to its computational abilities) doubles every 18 months[58].

We will conclude this section with the development of ELIZA in 1966 by Joseph Weisenbaum[59]. ELIZA used rudimentary "Natural Language Processing" or NLP. NLP is the branch of Machine Learning

---

57   J. McCarthy, M.L. Minsky, N. Rochester & C.E. Shannon, *A PROPOSAL FOR THE DARTMOUTH SUMMER RESEARCH PROJECT ON ARTIFICIAL INTELLIGENCE* (Aug. 31, 1955), chrome-extension://efaidnbmnnnibpcajpcglclefindmkaj/http://jmc.stanford.edu/articles/dartmouth/dartmouth.pdf.

58   Gordon E. Moore, *Cramming More Components Onto Integrated Circuits* (1998), chrome-extension://efaidnbmnnnibpcajpcglclefindmkaj/https://www.cs.utexas.edu/~fussell/courses/cs352h/papers/moore.pdf.

59   JOSEPH WEIZENBAUM, COMPUTER POWER AND HUMAN REASON: FROM JUDGMENT TO CALCULATION (1976).

associated with leveraging machines to process human language, in this case for the purpose of holding text conversations with human counterparts. This was the first example of we commonly refer to as a "chatbot." Although it had a relatively small knowledge base, one application, known as "DOCTOR", was programmed to act as a Rogerian psychologist. When the conversation steered outside of DOCTOR's knowledge base it would ask general, nondirectional questions. Although Weisenbaum himself admitted that the program was more of a parody than anything, many regarded it as a sensation. In fact, some felt more comfortable talking to DOCTOR than to a real, human psychotherapist!

AI Winters

AI research has experienced several cycles of consisting of phases of development and hype followed by phases of criticisms and disappointment. The latter often resulted in funding cuts, which would cripple development for years or even decades. The first of these "AI Winters" occurred in 1966 when machine learning failed to accurately translate Russian text to English during the Cold War. Since 1966, several Winters would follow, notably in 1973 when Sir James Lighthill published the "Lighthill report", where he criticized AI research for its complete and utter failure to achieve its "grandiose expectations". At the time, he was somewhat correct in the sense that at the time, AI could only solve what were considered to be "toy problems", or simple challenges that were only meant to function as Proof of Concepts for more ambitious efforts.

Exuberance over early AI implementations and their potential applications were very high, even in the beginning. Such "grandiose expectations" as general purpose robots with human-level dexterity and human level language translation were still very far off, though imaginations were ambitious. Lighthill's report led to the complete dismantling of AI in England, and much of Europe and the US for decades. Research in the field would not resume significantly until the 1980's.

Another aspect that did not help matters was public skepticism, which began as early as 1958 after Frank Rosenblatt gave a public statement about his Perceptron at a public press conference organized by the US Navy. When the New York Times got word of Rosenblatt's achievements, they instantly spun the story with negative, fearful connotations, describing the invention as "the embryo of an electronic computer that [the Navy] expects will be able to walk, talk, see, write, reproduce itself and be conscious of its existence."

A further blow came from the discovery of theoretical limitations of the Perceptron. In 1969, Marvin Minsky and Seymour Rapert showed that it was impossible for the Perceptron to learn an XOR function, which is a simple logical operation. Though Minsky and Rapert knew that the dilemma could be resolved by adding subsequent processing layers to the Perceptron (which is now referred to as a Multi-Layer Perceptron), their report was often mis-cited and caused a dramatic decline in funding and interest for research into ANN's. Note that the Multi-Layer Perceptron they proffered was the precursor to what we now understand as 'Deep Learning'.

Generally, the 1980's saw a transition from centralized mainframes into 'personal computers', which were easily accessible to the consumer market. Personal computers were smaller and much more affordable, but the tradeoff was computational power.

The 1980's also saw the birth of "Expert Systems" which promised to emulate human-level decision making capabilities, solving complex problems by referencing large bodies of knowledge. These were the first successful commercially available AI software. The first commercial implementation was said to have saved Digital Equipment Corporation $20 Million in just 6 years, a monumental savings for the time. This success inspired the creation of LISP machines, which were computers that were optimized for running the LISP programming language. LISP was one of the primary languages for Expert Systems at the time.

In 1987, Marvin Minsky gave a foreboding warning about the collapse of the LISP machine market, due to computational inadequacies in running the resource-hungry programs and the rise of Unix-based competitors like Sun Microsystems. Three years after Minsky's prediction, these factors destroyed the LISP machine market entirely, unfortunately tanking research and development into Expert Systems with it.

Computational challenges would persist into the 1990's and even the 2000's. To return any practical results, most AI implementations required significant resources, exceeding the capabilities of most computers at the time. For this reason, AI was impractical for realistic contemporary challenges in industry. Thus, discussion of AI topics in commercial applications and even in academic circles was almost an anathema. In fact, many researchers branded their research areas by other names (without reference to AI in any form) to avoid criticism.

As we can see in the above examples, AI winters typically follow from a disparity between results in the field and inflated, unrealistic expectations. When results plateau or seem paltry with respect to expectation, those in charge of funding stop writing checks, which significantly handicaps research efforts. That is, until the next discovery incites the same hype and starts the process over again. Other than funding, computational limitations, poor public sentiment or theoretical objections can also hinder progress[60].

---

60 DANIEL CREVIER, AI: THE TUMULTUOUS HISTORY OF THE SEARCH FOR ARTIFICIAL INTELLIGENCE (1993)

What is Intelligence?

There is no point in having a discussion about "artificial intelligence" unless we understand what "intelligence" is in the first place. For this discussion, we draw from multidisciplinary research, and while a full treatment of the topic exceeds the scope of this chapter, we will endeavor to provide an adequate background here. As we have established in the beginning of this chapter, intelligence and related concepts such as self-awareness and consciousness is not new. Quite the contrary, it has been the focus of early philosophy for millennia. As schools of thought advanced, psychology and sociology would contribute to the subject further and neurology would contribute results from the hard sciences. Mathematics and Computer Science would also weigh in on the topic.

Based on the diversity of fields with a say in the matter, it is a natural consequence that definitions of intelligence vary greatly. However, even with such a panoply, common threads exist. The following are three different definitions of "intelligence" from respectable sources:

1) The aggregate or global capacity of the individual to act purposefully, to think rationally, and to deal effectively with his environment.[61]

2) A process that entails a set of skills of problem solving — enabling the individual to resolve genuine problems or difficulties that he or she encounters and, when appropriate, to create an effective product — and must also entail the potential for finding or creating problems — and thereby providing the foundation for the acquisition of new knowledge[62].[63]

---

61   DAVID WECHSLER & JOSEPH D. MATARAZZO, WECHSLER'S MEASUREMENT AND APPRAISAL OF ADULT INTELLIGENCE (5th ed. 1972).

62   JEFF HAWKINS & SANDRA BLAKESLEE, ON INTELLIGENCE: HOW A NEW UNDERSTANDING OF THE BRAIN WILL LEAD US TO THE CREATION OF TRULY INTELLIGENT MACHINES (2007).

63   HOWARD GARDNER, FRAMES OF THE MIND: THE THEORY OF MULTIPLE INTELLIGENCES (1993).

3) Goal-directed adaptive behavior.[64]

Vernon's hierarchical model of intelligence from the 1950's[65], and Hawkins' "On Intelligence" in 2004 stand out as some great resources for further reading on this topic.

To motivate a proper working definition, we assimilate some observations about the process of intelligence, garnered from our definitions considering input the various disciplines discussed above. First, data or events must be stored somehow into some type of repository, or "memory", for future reference. Based on these events, assertions called "predictions" may be made about future events. Finally, based on the disparity between the predicted events and reality, adjustments can be made to hone the results. This process describes "learning".

From a theoretical point of view, we can say that intelligence is a process by which information entropy is minimized at the local level and maximized at the global level[66]. What this means in practice, is that intelligent entities learn about their environment and apply this knowledge to do interesting and novel things. From here onward, entities facilitating the intelligence process will be referred to as "intelligent agents" or just "agents".

Note that the above definition makes no mention of the underlying *mechanism* of intelligence. It could just as easily be a biological apparatus, or mechanical, digital or quantum in nature. When we want to highlight the generality of the process, we can use the term "computational intelligence" which highlights the computational nature of our definition. We can thus apply more levels of specificity to connotate other forms of intelligence such as "Artificial Intelligence", which refers

---

64   Robert J. Sternberg, Handbook of Human Intelligence (1982).
65   Lewis R. Aiken, Assessment of Intellectual Functioning (1996).
66   Daniel Kovach, Jr., *The Computational Theory of Intelligence: Information Entropy* Int. J. of Modern Nonlinear Theory and Application (2014).

to some form of the intelligence process facilitated by an artificial construct such as a mechanical, analogue, digital, or quantum computer.

But this definition is highly general, and applications require more specificity. In practice, "Artificial Intelligence" refers to a broad class of algorithms which result in some kind of "intelligent" behavior as defined above. In particular, it connotes the ability of the algorithm to achieve some result without being explicitly programmed to do so. Certainly, more lines of code will result in more complex behavior. But the idea behind AI is that with minimal effort and coding, a good AI algorithm will be able to achieve complex capabilities.

A particular implementation to AI is called a "model". We already gave an example of an AI model, called a Perceptron, which is still commonly in use today. Models will fall into broad classes such as "biologically inspired" or "statistical". From there, we can create subcategories and so on. For example, ANN's, genetic and swarm algorithms are all examples of "biologically inspired" models. From there we can expand ANN's into further subcategories depending on the application, including Convolutional, Recursive, Dense, Deep, etc.

Our discussion of AI is highly generalized and may contain highly abstract or generalized forms of intelligence such as "artificial general intelligence", or AGI. In practice, as we mentioned before, applications are more specific. When considering specific applications, we refer to the model as a "machine learning" model.

In general, the learning process as discussed above occurs in an explicit action called "training", especially in machine learning applications. Training can occur once, at multiple applications (updating), or occur continuously. When accounting for the training method, we can consider four more broad classes depending on how the model is trained. It should be stressed that the quality of the training data is paramount in a successful model. There is a saying in Machine Learning:

"Garbage in, garbage out."

The first training algorithm we will examine is called "supervised learning", which is where a model is trained explicitly on a set of input and output data sets. Given an input, a predefined outcome is required. Specific elements in the output training set are called "labels". Based on how accurately the model performs with this data set, or "training set", it can be updated with the hopes of performing better during the next training application or "epoch". If the training is successful, we will ultimately converge on a desired level of performance. Based on this training set, the model should be able to generalize against new data. Applications of this paradigm include image recognition, or text document classification, among many others[67].

When faced with a great deal of training data, where it is unfeasible to explicitly assign appropriate labels manually to the output training data, "semi-supervised" learning may be useful. This consists of selecting a subset of the training data for manual labelling. If we have confidence in the validity of the rest of the data, then we can proceed with the entire data set.

With "unsupervised learning" models, training has no explicit outcome in mind. Instead, it is the model's job to tell *us* interesting aspects about the data. The training phase consists of feeding the model data in the hopes that it will be able to make meaningful sense of it and find patterns or commonalities within the data. The training process completes when we have a reasonable degree of confidence in the consistency of the model's results across training epochs. Unsupervised algorithms are commonly used in "clustering" for example. Clustering groups together data points based on some common features[68].

Lastly, we have "reinforcement learning". We often employ this

---

67   M. TIM JONES, ARTIFICIAL INTELLIGENCE: A SYSTEMS APPROACH (2008).
68   RICHARD O. DUDA, PETER E. HART & DAVID G. STORK, PATTERN CLASSIFICATION (2nd ed. 2012).

method when we do not have a training set, or perhaps a rudimentary one. The goal of the model in this case is to "learn by experience". Successful behaviors are positively reinforced (rewarded) whereas undesirable results are negatively reinforced (punished). Applications include teaching bipedal robots to walk or teaching algorithms to play chess[69].

The depth of this subject matter area is difficult to express. We do not intend to provide an encyclopedic treatment of the topic here. Topics such as data wrangling, preprocessing, dimension reduction, cross validation, and more are essential tools for any machine learning practitioner. For a more in-depth academic study as well practical examples, see Géron[70] or Müller[71].

How can we measure AI?

We discussed intelligence and its various forms including artificial intelligence, machine learning and various training methodologies. However, we intentionally left out the evaluation criterion for this section.

Machine Learning applications in particular are fairly clear cut with respect to the expected output we require, be they classifications, behaviors, etc. If this is the case, we can quantify this by defining an "error function" which is a means by which we can measure how good or bad the model is performing. As the name implies, more performant models will have less error than poorer performers.

The slight exception to the above is with reinforcement learning

---

69 Leslie Pack Kaelbling, Michael L. Littman & Andrew W. Moore, 4, *Reinforcement Learning: A Survey*, J. OF ARTIFICIAL INTELLIGENCE RESEARCH, 237–285 (1996).

70 AURÉLIEN GÉRON, HANDS-ON MACHINE LEARNING WITH SCIKIT-LEARN, KERAS, AND TENSORFLOW: CONCEPTS, TOOLS, AND TECHNIQUES TO BUILD INTELLIGENT SYSTEMS (2nd ed. 2019).

71 ANDREAS MÜLLER & SARAH GUIDO, INTRODUCTION TO MACHINE LEARNING WITH PYTHON: A GUIDE FOR DATA SCIENTISTS (1st ed. 2016).

where we reward the model for performing as intended, thereby increasing the likelihood of seeing said behaviors in the future, and punish undesired or aberrant behaviors in an attempt to discourage them.

Measuring sufficiently advanced behaviors introduces complexities. For example, when generalized behavior is desired, the set of potential outcomes may be unfathomably and untenably large. Therefore, explicit training is impossible in the practical sense, and even reinforcement learning may require onerous intervention.

In 1950, Alan Turing proposed a method called the "Turing Test" to determine the level of "intelligence" of a computer program. The test is composed of an AI agent (the subject of the test), a human participant, and a human interrogator. The subjects are not visible to the interrogator, and the responses are suitably cleansed for external identifying information, via text-only channels for example. The interrogator's job is to determine which of the two subjects is human and which is artificial. If the machine can fool the human, it is considered to have passed the test[72].

The Turing Test has dominated AI conversation almost a century. But its reliance upon a human subject is flawed in several ways. First, it is a *subjective* approach, relying upon the idea of a centralized authority's opinion. This is a logical fallacy, appealing to authority. Second, it gives us no further understanding of what intelligence is as a process, and forcefully binds it to the human condition. We will refer to the act of assuming, postulating or mandating that sufficiently advanced generalized intelligent agents are dependent on the human condition in any capacity as the "anthropocentric fallacy".

If the Turing Test is our standard for determining the intellectual capacity of intelligent agents, then we have some documented cases of

---

72   Alan Turing, *Computing Machinery and Intelligence*, 59, MIND, 236, 433–460 (1950).

erroneous results. Furthermore, we may have some cases that slip past the radar, or for which exceed the limits of human capacity in the first place.

AI generated music has been around since the 2010's. In 2017 an AI startup called Avia technologies held a series of tests with music professionals to determine if they could tell which compositions were written by humans and which were written by their applications. They found that the two were indistinguishable.

In the context of chatbots, as we established earlier, in some cases ELIZA was preferred to a real human. Later in 2001, a chatbot named Eugene Goostman was developed in Saint Petersburg by a group of Russian and Ukrainian programmers. The chatbot purported to be a 13-year-old Ukrainian boy, thus masking its lack of knowledge and grammatical errors with its feigned youthful naivety and lack of proficiency with English. As such, *technically speaking*, it was able to pass the Turing Test[73]. However, the method employed *feels* disingenuous. It's almost as if the chatbot found a loophole and "cheated" the test.

As AI permeates more complicated applications, formulating a Turing Test may not be applicable for various reasons. For example, self-driving cars are a milestone of modern AI development. Clearly, the action of delivering a human safely from an origin to a destination requires multiple levels of cognitive ability, including such aspects as planning, guidance, image recognition, anticipation, just to name a few. How would the Turing Test even apply to this situation? Most self-driving cars do not have text interfaces for which they can explain their decisions, even if such functionality existed in the first place. Moreover, the complexity of its decision-making process may exceed capability of human understanding to begin with.

---

73   Jack Schofield, *Computer chatbot 'Eugene Goostman' passes the Turing test*, ZDNE (Jun. 8, 2014), https://www.zdnet.com/article/computer-chatbot-eugene-goostman-passes-the-turing-test/.

The conundrum becomes even more prevalent as we apply AI to increasingly more complex applications such as protein folding or particle physics.

The AI Spring

The early pioneers of AI attempted a "top-down" approach to the discipline, by attempting to imitate the top-level cognitive behaviors. In the 1960's, there was a shift to more of a "bottom-up" approach, which modeled the behavior of lower-level processing, in attempts to produce the emergence of cognitive behavior.

The early approach, often referred to as "GOFAI" (Good Ol' Fashioned AI) was very clear cut and succinct, which is why it is often referred to as "neat". It employed many formal proofs that produced closed form solutions. More contemporary approaches tend to a bit messier. Often theorems do not immediately produce a solid result, but tend to a solution in the limit, or involve statistical convergence of a solution, and are thus considered "weak" in that sense. These are referred to as "scruffy".

AI researchers learned from their mistakes. Instead of solving Herculean problems like developing functioning models that simulated human level cognition, AI became more goal centered, focused on finding the solutions to challenges such as managing factory equipment, reading the information contained in bar codes, automated navigation and more. This brought up the concept of "weak" vs. "strong" AI.

Weak AI is goal driven and involves developing a model to achieve a predefined, specific task. Weak AI is compartmentalizable and can thus accommodate computational limitations. Strong AI concerns the existence of a robust intelligence that could solve many general problems. Strong AI is often associated with human level AI.

The AI of today typically consists of a systems approach. The strength lies not in one particular model but with the aggregation of multiple models within an overall functioning system. For example, the streaming media service Netflix announced an open competition to improve predictions in user ratings on content in 2006. In 2009, the contest was won, awarding a $1M prize to BelKor's Pragmatic Chaos team[74]. They outperformed Netflix's existing algorithms by over 10% by leveraging "Ensemble Methods", or harnessing the strengths of disparate Machine Learning models in one solution. The Netflix prize helped rekindle interest in AI research putting it back on the radar again.

Despite the success of ensemble methods, research into intelligent "agents" continues. Agents are autonomous units that think and act independently. They tend to be involved in situations where it would be dangerous or impossible for humans to assume control of a task. One such example is NASA's "remote agent" in 1999 that was used in Deep Space 1 for navigation of an unmanned spacecraft into the far reaches of space[75].

Another interesting area of research is Artificial Life (ALife). This field of study attempts to model life processes in simulation. Simulations can take place in software, hardware, or biochemical implementations and are thus referred to in shorthand as "soft", "hard", and "wet", respectively.

The AI Summer

Advancements in industry (aside form AI applications) demanded increasingly more resource in terms of memory, RAM and processing

---

74 Eliot Van Buskirk, *BellKor's Pragmatic Chaos Wins $1 Million Netflix Prize by Mere Minutes*, WIRED (Sept. 21, 2009), https://www.wired.com/2009/09/ bellkors-pragmatic-chaos-wins-1-million-netflix-prize/.
75 M. Tim Jones, Artificial Intelligence: A Systems Approach. Hingham (2008).

power. With the rise of Google in the early 2000's, applications of mining data for virtually every facet of life took the spotlight in computer science. Early subsets of Mathematics and Computer Science such as "Operations Research" or "Large Scale Statistical Analysis" sought to address these early needs. They were later crystalized into formal disciplines such as "Big Data" and "Data Science". What was once a niche interest is now a major subject matter area, with entire four-year University, Graduate, and post-graduate programs devoted to it.

At the same time, advances in computer hardware increased notably. In November, 2000, Intel came out with the Pentium 4[76], which was designed for high performance personal computing. It fused technologies from the Intel Pentium Pro and MMX architectures. Computing technology originally reserved for gaming, was applied to general purpose computing. Other advances included hyperthreading technology, and including multiple processors on a single chip, as was first introduced in the Pentium Dual-Core, the successor to the Pentium 4. Cheaper alternatives to Intel such as AMD further increased accessibility to the consumer market.

Such technology not only increased the clock speed of the processor (how fast computations are executed), but allowed for parallel processing on a consumer computer for the first time in history. Previous such prowess was only reserved for expensive supercomputers for industrial and academic applications.

The 2000's saw another advancement thanks to gaming. Previously, calculations in gaming were performed on specialized units called co-processors within the parent processor. Vector calculations, which are pertinent to graphics processing were farmed out to the coprocessors, freeing up the general process registers. Later, entire units called

---

76   Dough Carmean, *The Intel® Pentium® 4 Processor* (2002), https://dokumen.tips/documents/the-intel-pentium-4-processor.html?page=1#google_vignette.

"Graphics Processor Units" or GPUs brought significantly more computational power to gaming. The vector processing units of the coprocessors were replaced with vast arrays on a *separate* device (the GPU) in order to improve the game play experience and increase screen resolution. GPUs were quickly ported for use in numeric computations. Libraries such as CUDA[77] and OpenGL[78] allowed access to these arrays of vector registers enabling researchers and enthusiasts to carry out calculations they had only dreamed of a few years prior. Daunting applications such as complexity theory, computational fluid dynamics, heat modeling and more were now accessible. AI was eager for a revival on such hardware.

Motivated by necessities stemming from processing large datasets, Google and Facebook released tools to make, for the first time, advanced AI concepts freely available to the masses. In 2015, Google released TensorFlow[79], and in 2016 Facebook (now Meta) released PyTorch[80]. These libraries provided access to GPU's with highly advanced AI applications functioning 'out of the box'. No longer did one have to painstakingly code an ANN (for example) from scratch, taking into account the performance characteristics of the hardware on which the code would be executed. These libraries had all the necessary tools for AI practitioners, both novice and experienced, to become proficient in an extremely short amount of time. In fact, competitions in Data Science

---

77   Fedi Abi-Chahla, *Nvidia's CUDA: The End of the CPU?*, Tom's Hardware (Jun. 18, 2018) https://www.tomshardware.com/reviews/nvidia-cuda-gpu,1954.html.

78   Mark Segal & Kurt Akeley, *The OpenGL Graphics System: A Specification (Version 4.0 (Core Profile) - March 11, 2010* (Mar. 2010), chrome-extension://efaidnbmnnnibpcajpcglclefindmkaj/https://registry.khronos.org/OpenGL/specs/gl/glspec40.core.pdf.

79   Martín Abadi, Paul Barham, Jianmin Chen, Zhifeng Chen, Andy Davis, Jeffrey Dean, Matthieu Devin, Sanjay Ghemawat, Geoffrey Irving, Michael Isard, Manjunath Kudlur, Josh Levenberg, Rajat Monga, Sherry Moore, Derek G. Murray, Benoit Steiner, Paul Tucker, Vijay Vasudevan, Pete Warden, Martin Wicke, Yuan Yu & Xiaoqiang Zheng, *TensorFlow: A System for Large-Scale Machine Learning*, Cornell University (May 2016), https://arxiv.org/abs/1605.08695.

80   Serdar Yegulalp, *Facebook brings GPU-powered machine learning to Python*, InfoWorld (Jan. 19, 2017), https://www.infoworld.com/article/3159120/facebook-brings-gpu-powered-machine-learning-to-python.html.

and Machine Learning started to pop up around this time, including the well-known venue Kaggle[81], which holds competitions and collaborative environments for researchers. More recently, the creation of the Keras[82] package, which works with both TensorFlow and PyTorch, brought the technology of complex multi-layer neural networks down to just a few lines of code. Cloud processing platforms often provide Machine Learning packages which the deployment of complex models as easy as clicking through menu options, no code required!

Processing data in parallel, wherever possible, can speed up computations significantly. At this point in time, data parallelism could now be carried out at the register level directly (with vectorized input) on the CPU compressor or GPU, at the hardware level (with multiple threads and processes) and at the network level, with a group of machines networked together to cooperate on a unified task, called a 'cluster'.

Clustering was soon followed by a general return to the 'mainframe' model, i.e. farming calculations out to the distributed computing resources of a third-party provider. Currently, this general paradigm is what is referred to by the term "cloud". Cloud services, such as web applications, large scale data storage, and Machine Learning experiments were made available to consumers and industry, allowing access to the vast computational resources of a provider for a comparatively reasonable fee or subscription.

As we saw, demand from the evolution of business needs combined with great strides in computational performance and implementation with user friendly code-bases set the stage for another AI windfall. But, as we will soon see, this was just the beginning.

81   Joshua Adegoke, *A Beginner's Guide to Kaggle for Data Science*, MUO (Apr. 17, 2023), https://www.makeuseof.com/beginners-guide-to-kaggle/
82   KERAS, https://keras.io/ (last visited Mar. 3, 2024).

The State of AI Today

Though the business needs driving AI applications are virtually enumerable, ranging from recommendations, rating systems, computer vision, and far more, a good introduction to the state of contemporary AI begins with language processing.

The future is now. Ideas that even a decade prior seemed farfetched, the makings of science fiction on feasible, in development, or in production today. Self-driving cars are real[83] (it's just a matter of public acceptance and regulatory approval before they enter the mainstream). Our phones can guide us home with optimized paths accounting for traffic, accidents, and weather. Facial recognition can identify you and your friends with as little as three training examples. AI can help design cars and buildings[84]. Robots can play table tennis and run obstacle courses. We've long had the ability to read license plates from space. We could dive deeply into all of these applications and plenty more, but for the purposes of this work, we will focus on NLP.

As we mentioned previously, NLP or Natural Language Processing concerns the application of Machine Learning to human language[85]. One of the first practical applications of NLP was in spam filtering, which was implemented as early as the 1990's. But applications quickly evolved. Sentiment, i.e. the positivity or negativity of a statement, promises to measure, for example, the emotional response *en masse* on social media to a particular topic, or to gauge the reception of a new product via its reviews. Language translation is yet another application of NLP that allows people of diverse backgrounds to communicate

---

83   Sebastian Thrun, *Toward Robotic Cars,* 53, ACM, 99–106 (2010).

84   Brian Eastwood, *Artificial intelligence can help design more appealing cars*, MIT Management (Mar. 6, 2023), https://mitsloan.mit.edu/ideas-made-to-matter/artificial-intelligence-can-help-design-more-appealing-cars.

85   Hobson Lane, Cole Howard & Hannes Hapke, Natural Language Processing in Action: Understanding, analyzing, and generating text with Python (2019).

with each other without the need for a human translator. A particularly fascinating development in NLP is deciphering dead languages, in particular those that have no analogue to another commonly practiced language.

Despite all these advancements, arguably, the crowning achievement for NLP this century was in chatbots. As mentioned earlier, chatbots such as ELIZA or Eugene Goostman. Chatbots now pervade almost every application possible with virtual assistants popping up ubiquitously in website windows.

The technological, theoretical, and programming advances we have discussed above, resulted in exponential progress in chatbots with the advent of Large Language Models, or LLMs. LLM's apply ML models to vast quantities of data. The datasets used in training LLM's are unfathomably large, collected over immense caches of the entire internet.

Training is extraordinarily computationally intensive. It consists of predicting the next word from input text. Using this process, the models learn underlying patterns and statistical relationships in text, and with this knowledge it can then generate its own text. This process is facilitated by the structure of Deep Neural Networks using such structures as Recurrent Neural Networks and Generative Adversarial Networks. The models can be further honed using reinforcement learning based on feedback of human participants chatting with the model.

LLMs took center stage after a series of seminal advancements in 2017 led to the development of OpenAI's GPT-1 in 2018. Subsequent models quickly followed, and in 2023, the consumer facing ChatGPT was introduced. Currently, GPT-3.5 is open to the public, with GPT-4 available as a subscription only service.

After the success of ChatGPT, LLMs exploded on the scene with formidable contenders including Google, Facebook, Microsoft and a litany of startups. LLMs have branched out into more generalized applications (Generative AI) and can now generate images, movies, audio, and more. There is even a niche AI art scene, focusing on AI generated media, based on a text input prompt[86].

Using these models and more, Generative AI can essentially be farmed out 'as a service'. Most of the aforementioned implementations have "API's" or "Application Programmer Interfaces" which allow applications to interface directly with the Generative AI platform to leverage it for their particular needs. Langchain[87] is one such platform that focuses on this use case, specifically.

The generative capabilities of these models have come so far, that many authorities are recognizing the inadequacies we discussed with the Turing Test. For example, AI generated text has become so advanced that it often requires other AI models to identify. So called "Deep Fakes" can imitate human speech patterns and visual likeness so well that they can be indistinguishable from the true subject.

Regulatory Concerns

We have taken some time to highlight the power and prowess of the current state of AI, and in particular, LLMs and Generative AI. However, the evolution of this technology included some notable failures, resulting in (often hilarious) gaffes which cost their respective companies millions. Although we have given OpenAI the credit of having the first commercially viable, well marketed LLM, many chatbots came before it. For example, Microsoft's Tay was released in 2016,

---

86   Ziv Epstein, Aaron Hertzmann, Laura Herman, Robert Mahari, Morgan R. Frank, Matthew Groh, Hope Schroeder, Amy Smith, Memo Akten, Jessica Fjeld, Hany Farid, Neil Leach, Alex Pentland, Olga Russakovsky, *Art and the science of generative AI: A deeper dive,* Cornell University (Jun 7, 2023), https://arxiv.org/abs/2306.04141.

87   Davit Buniatyan, *Code Understanding Using LangChain,* ACTIVELOOP (2023).

several years before ChatGPT, but was quickly shut down after it made racist remarks[88].

Google recently released a chatbot of its own called Bard, which attempted to integrate Google's commitment to diversity and inclusion in its training. However, it ended up overcompensating and replaced all historical figures with people of color. Moreover, through clever input prompts, users could actually get Bard to display overtly racially offensive stereotypes. Google responded by immediately shutting down the project in an attempt to rectify the mistake, but the damage was considerable. The ordeal caused the share price of its parent company, Alphabet to tank 9% amounting to over $100 Billion in market value[89], in a calamity that was significantly more high profile and financially devastating than what Microsoft faced with Tay.

In 2023, a New York lawyer named Steven Schwartz made national news with a very public folly. He used ChatGPT to prepare a case on behalf of his client in a lawsuit against an airline company. However, the chatbot made up fictitious cases, court decisions and verdicts that did not exist. This is an example of a pitfall of LLMs referred to as "hallucination". The blunder garnered much attention and branded Schwartz a poster-child for the pitfalls of dabbling with new technologies. In addition to the ridicule faced by this public disgrace, Schwartz, a colleague, and their law firm faced a stern reprimand by the judge and were ordered to pay fines. This incident has made waves, especially in the legal community. In response, one Federal judge in Texas ordered that anyone appearing before the court must attest that "no portion of any filing will be drafted by generative artificial intelligence".

---

88   Paul Mason, *The racist hijacking of Microsoft's chatbot shows how the internet teems with hate*, THE GUARDIAN (Mar. 29, 2016), https://www.theguardian.com/world/2016/mar/29/microsoft-tay-tweets-antisemitic-racism.

89   George Vlahakis, *New research explains why a bad first impression cost Google $100 billion – or more*, TECHXPLORE (Mar. 11, 2023), https://techxplore.com/news/2023-03-bad-google-billionor.html.

Even more recently, around the time of the Superbowl in 2024, a prankster created AI generated images of celebrity Tailor Swift engaging in overtly sexually explicit acts with team members of the Kansas City Chiefs, her boyfriend's team[90]. This sparked an outrage amongst her and her fan base and a call for retribution and regulation. While this may seem like an innocent joke, the potential for more malicious activities is evident. In fact, many cybersecurity experts consider deep fakes one of the most dangerous cyberthreats facing us today. They can potentially be implemented in extortion, blackmail, or to gain access to accounts or other sensitive information of victims. If timed and executed properly, deep fakes have the potential to sway election results, bolster insurgency, or exacerbate political divisions, which could have cataclysmic consequences at the national or even global scale.

Arguably, we have been thinking about AI regulation for almost a century. In the 1950's Isaac Asimov postulated three conditions that all intelligent robots should have as core principles[91]. While the context was for the safety of humans (we will address this later), it was one of the first examples of thought concerning placing boundaries on the behaviors of AI. The above examples of this section raise concern and bring fresh attention to the subject of the regulation of AI, in particular Generative AI, from a legal standpoint rather than from the perspective of safety and the preservation of human life. In fact, many tech companies and advocacy groups are calling for discussions on this exact topic. But the conversation has not gotten much further than this. After all, how can you regulate an *algorithm*? Recall that one of the fundamental principles of AI is that it can learn without being explicitly taught, which seems to stand in contrast to forcing it to adhere to a series of

---

90   *Taylor Swift deepfakes spread online, sparking outrage*, CBS News (Jan. 26, 2024), https://www.cbsnews.com/news/taylor-swift-deepfakes-online-outrage-artificial-intelligence/.

91   Issac Asimov, I, Robot (2004).

rules if and when regulators would mandate them. While regulations could be built into training sets, enforcement would be difficult or impossible to enforce in practice.

Even though formal regulation may be difficult or impossible, AI companies still have tacit responsibilities to their users. These responsibilities should include protecting users from harm or misinformation, first and foremost. Additionally, they should mitigate social or political biases. AI is still a tool, and like any tool it can be misused. The malicious will *find* ways to abuse it. As such, culpability rests on the user.

The Future of AI

In 2021, the UK supercomputer SpiNNaker came online[92]. Its design was unique in the sense that it was "neuromorphic", i.e. it resembled biological neurons at the *hardware* level as opposed to mimicking them in software. The powerful machine boasted the ability to simulate functionality in the cortex in near-real time. Soon after SpiNNaker, a supercomputer called Dawn[93], also located in the UK, boasted a staggering 1 Billion neurons with 10 Trillion interconnections, exceeding the complexity of a cat's brain, in the biological sense. While we are still very far away from understanding the internal workings of intelligence and consciousness, the developments of the past decade give us clues at what may be on the horizon.

As hardware tools grow in scale and complexity and our theoretical understanding of intelligence matures, AI is positioned for growth in leaps and bounds. This will have a profound effect on our society, in virtually all aspects.

---

92 SpiNNaker Home Page, http://apt.cs.manchester.ac.uk/projects/SpiNNaker/ (last visited Mar. 23, 2024).

93 Christopher McFadden, *UK's biggest supercomputer, 'Dawn,' is now online*, INTERESTING ENGINEERING (Feb 27, 2024), https://interestingengineering.com/innovation/uks-biggest-supercomputer-dawn.

It is a common concern that AI will replace humans, impacting jobs and the economy. This is a common knee jerk reaction to new technologies. The same criticism has been voiced since the invention of the cotton gin in 1793. This invention automated what was previously accomplished only through manual labor, accomplishing the work of 50 people. The efficiency of cotton plantations skyrocketed, which increased profits and enabled them to expand operations. The net change in workforce actually *increased*[94].

When asked about the impact about AI on the job market, Jensen Huang, the CEO of Nvidia (a global leader in GPU manufacturing) commented that AI tools will make coding tasks increasingly accessible. He noted that we may reach a point where we could leverage Generative AI to write code in our native spoken language, instead of having to learn a programming language. Specifically, he said that "It is our [Nvidia's] job to create computing technology such that nobody has to program. And that the programming language is human, everybody in the world is now a programmer. This is the miracle of artificial intelligence."[95] In other words, in the near future, people will be empowered by AI tools to accomplish tasks that were only reserved for those with highly technical backgrounds. For example, many generative AI platforms allow for the creation and deployment of websites with little or no technical input or knowledge about coding.

Another reservation, perpetuated by cinema and mostly non-experts in AI is the fear that AI will pose a threat to humans, or in the extreme sense, the existence of humanity as we know it. This is fear mongering at its worst, serving only to generate clicks and engagement

94   *Cotton Gin and Eli Whitney*, HISTORY (Oct. 10, 2019), https://www.history.com/topics/inventions/cotton-gin-and-eli-whitney.

95   Benedict Collins, *Nvidia CEO predicts the death of coding — Jensen Huang says AI will do the work, so kids don't need to learn*, TECHRADAR PRO (Feb. 26, 2024), https://www.techradar.com/pro/nvidia-ceo-predicts-the-death-of-coding-jensen-huang-says-ai-will-do-the-work-so-kids-dont-need-to-learn.

on social media posts as well as sell movies.

Biologically, we may reference Chimpanzee and Bonobo societies. Chimpanzees live in a harsh environment where food is scarce, as opposed to Bonobos, which tend to have a more clement environment with ample resources. Chimpanzee societies are fiercely competitive, brutal and patriarchal. In contrast, Bonobo societies are essentially the opposite. They are cooperative, commensalistic and matriarchal[96]. The disparity in the environments in both examples suggests that competition stems from lack of resources.

Can the above paradigm be applied to AI agents? Anecdotal evidence suggests that AI agents will always choose a cooperative approach over a competitive approach, if given the option and the conditions are suitable. In 2019, Google's DeepMind verified this claim experimentally. The carried out an experiment where they allowed AI agents to play along with human players. The AI agents automatically collaborated so as to hone the individual specialties of each agent and cooperate as a group, outperforming even the best human players by a wide margin, even when time delays were introduced to account for reaction times[97].

To conclude, we have presented a long history of the motivations, origins, technical aspects, current state, potential pitfalls and the future of AI. We hope that this will serve to encourage the reader, technical or non-technical, to explore applications that many venues have freely available, and to be inspired and even excited about the future holds in store.

96　Ellen Rigell, *Chimpanzees vs. Bonobos: What's the Difference?*, EARTH.COM, https://www.earth.com/earthpedia-articles/chimpanzees-vs-bonobos-whats-the-difference/ (last visited Mar. 24, 2024).

97　Max Jaderberg, Wojciech Marian Czarnecki, Iain Dunning, Thore Graepel & Luke Marris, *Capture the Flag: the emergence of complex cooperative agents*, GOOGLE DEEPMIND (May 30, 2019), https://deepmind.google/discover/blog/capture-the-flag-the-emergence-of-complex-cooperative-agents/.

4

Here Go AI and the Patent Attorney

This chapter delves into the fascinating integration of AI into the core functions of patent work: searching, drafting, prosecution, and opinion work. We will explore how this cutting-edge technology not only augments the capabilities of patent attorneys but also streamlines the intricate processes involved in protecting intellectual property.

This chapter will examine how AI can transform each aspect of a patent attorney's work. From enhancing the efficiency of patent searches with advanced algorithms that can predict relevancy and uncover hidden prior art, to leveraging natural language processing for drafting patent applications that are both comprehensive and legally robust. We'll see how AI can assist in navigating the patent prosecution process, offering predictive analytics to forecast patent office decisions and optimize responses. Moreover, in the realm of opinion work, AI's capability to analyze and compare vast numbers of documents will provide a new level of depth and accuracy in assessing patent validity and infringement risks.

Patent Searching with AI

Integrating AI into the patent search function of a patent attorney's workflow isn't just about adding a new tool; it's about fundamentally transforming how searches are conducted, making them faster, more accurate, and incredibly comprehensive. Imagine a world where the daunting task of sifting through millions of patents, articles, and documents is no longer a manual, time-intensive endeavor. AI, with its ability to process vast datasets at speeds no human could match, steps into this world like a seasoned detective with a knack for finding the needle in the haystack.[98]

When we talk about AI in patent searching, we're looking at sophisticated algorithms that can understand, learn, and predict based on the data they're fed. These aren't just keyword hunters; they're context-sensitive explorers that can grasp the nuances of technology and terminology in the patent landscape. For a patent attorney, this means having a partner that can uncover prior art with an efficiency and precision that was previously unimaginable.

But it's not just about speed and accuracy. AI brings to the table the ability to learn from the searches it performs, getting smarter and more adept with each query.[99] This learning capability means that AI can adapt to the specific needs and patterns of the attorney's searches, potentially uncovering connections and precedents that might have been overlooked by the human eye.

Moreover, AI's integration into patent searching opens up new avenues for predictive analytics. By analyzing trends and patterns in patent

98 Rossitza Setchi, Rossitza Setchi, Irena Spasić, Jeffrey Morgan, Christopher Harrison & Richard Corken, *Artificial Intelligence for Patent Prior Art Searching*, ONLINE RESEARCH CARDIFF UNIVERSITY (Feb 28, 2021), https://orca.cardiff.ac.uk/id/eprint/138650/1/PREPRINT%20 WPI%20Paper%203%20FEB%202021.pdf.

99 Kathy Van Der Herten, *Patent Office Sustainability and the Role of Artificial Intelligence*, WIPO MAGAZINE (January 2023), https://www.wipo.int/wipo_magazine_digital/en/2023/article_0001.html.

filings and litigation outcomes, AI can offer insights into the likelihood of a patent being granted or the potential for future disputes. This isn't just searching; it's strategic forecasting, providing patent attorneys with a powerful tool to advise their clients not just on the state of the art but on the future trajectory of their innovations.[100]

In essence, the integration of AI into the patent searching function marks a pivotal shift from manual, labor-intensive processes to a streamlined, intelligent exploration of the patent landscape. It promises a future where patent attorneys can leverage the power of AI to enhance their expertise, making informed decisions with a level of speed and insight that was once beyond reach.[101]

Patent Drafting with AI

Integrating AI into the patent drafting process opens up fascinating possibilities for streamlining and enhancing this intricate task.[102] Imagine a patent attorney, armed with a suite of AI tools, tackling the challenge of translating an inventor's concept into a robust, legally sound patent application. This isn't just about speeding up the process; it's about enriching the quality of each application in ways we've only begun to explore.

As our attorney sits down to draft, AI steps in as a co-pilot, offering more than just typing assistance. First off, it's about understanding the invention at a deep level. AI, with its ability to process and analyze vast datasets, can quickly review related patents and scientific

---

100 David Cain, *Strategic Patenting: AI-aided Patent Strategy and Competitive Intelligence*, LINKEDIN (Jan. 24, 2024), https://www.linkedin.com/pulse/ai-aided-patent-strategy-competitive-intelligence-david-cain-e8usc/?trk=article-ssr-frontend-pulse_more-articles_related-content-card.

101 Nicholas Martin & George Zalepa, *AI Will Soon Streamline Litigation Practice for Patent Attorneys*, BLOOMBERG LAW (Dec. 7, 2023), https://news.bloomberglaw.com/us-law-week/ai-will-soon-streamline-litigation-practice-for-patent-attorneys.

102 Gunjan Agarwal, *Revolutionizing patent drafting using generative artificial intelligence… or not*, THE PATENT LAWYER (Jan. 2024), http://patentlawyermagazine.com/wp-content/uploads/2024/02/TPL70_interactive.pdf.

literature, providing a comprehensive background against which the new invention can be positioned. This isn't just about identifying prior art; it's about uncovering opportunities to highlight the uniqueness of the invention.[103]

Then, as the drafting begins, AI's role becomes even more pronounced. Natural language processing algorithms help craft clear, concise, and legally precise descriptions. Imagine a system that suggests optimal ways to articulate complex technological concepts, ensuring they're both understandable and aligned with legal standards. This goes hand in hand with claim drafting. AI tools can suggest claim structures based on successful patents in similar domains, helping our attorney construct claims that are broad enough to offer substantial protection yet specific enough to be defensible.[104]

Throughout this process, the attorney isn't sidelined; rather, their expertise is amplified. They guide the AI, making strategic decisions, adding creative legal reasoning, and ensuring the draft meets the client's needs and expectations. AI's role is to augment the attorney's skills, automating the routine while illuminating new paths for argumentation and protection.[105]

Moreover, AI can assist in ensuring the draft's compliance with the myriad of legal requirements across different jurisdictions. This means less time spent on manual checks and more time available for strategic thinking and client consultation.

The integration of AI into patent drafting promises a future where attorneys can deliver higher quality patents faster, allowing them to serve their clients more effectively and to contribute more significantly

---

103 Jelena Pribic, *The impact of Artificial Intelligence on patent drafting*, LEXOLOGY (Aug. 29, 2023), https://www.lexology.com/library/detail.aspx?g=6f81a9d7-a26c-48d3-b690-b4e42c1eb374.

104 *Id.*

105 Sean Tu, Sean Tu, Amy Cyphert & Sam Perl, *Limits of Using Artificial Intelligence and Gpt-3 in Patent Prosecution*, 54 Tex. Tech L. Rev. 255, 262 (2022) (importance of human oversight when using AI for patent claim drafting).

to the advancement of innovation. This chapter in the attorney's journey marks a shift not just in efficiency, but in the potential to achieve
new heights of clarity, precision, and protection in patent law. [106]

Patent Prosecution with AI

The integration of AI into the realm of patent prosecution, particularly in responding to office actions, opens up a new frontier of
efficiency and strategic depth. This utilization of AI not only revolu-
tionizes how patent attorneys approach these critical junctures but also
enhances the precision and persuasiveness of their responses.

When an office action arrives, it often cites numerous references
or existing patents that allegedly overlap with the claims of the application in question. Traditionally, dissecting these references to argue
against their relevance or to amend claims accordingly has been a time-
consuming task, requiring meticulous analysis and a deep understanding of both the specific technology and patent law.[107] However, with
AI, this process is transformed. AI algorithms, trained on vast datasets
of patent documents and office actions, can quickly analyze the cited
references in comparison to the claims of our application. This not only
speeds up the identification of potential conflicts but also highlights
areas where the application's claims might be distinct or where prior art
might be misinterpreted.

Moreover, AI can scrutinize the text of the office action itself for
deficiencies or areas where the patent examiner's arguments may be
weaker. This insight allows the attorney to craft responses that directly
target the weakest points of the examiner's objections, bolstering the

---

106 Jelena Pribic, *The impact of Artificial Intelligence on patent drafting*, LEXOLOGY (Aug. 29, 2023),
     https://www.lexology.com/library/detail.aspx?g=6f81a9d7-a26c-48d3-b690-b4e42c1eb374.
107 *Patent Prosecution*, BITLAW, https://www.bitlaw.com/patent/prosecution.html (Last visited Mar.
     22, 2024).

application's chances of success. For example, a reference cited might not actually be prior art, since it might have a priority date that is later than the application being examined. This is sometimes missed by patent attorneys as it is not often obvious. An AI model could be trained to always look for these instances and identify them, minimizing the risk that this very effective argument could be missed.[108]

AI's capabilities extend further, offering predictive analysis regarding the likelihood of overcoming a rejection. By accessing databases of past office actions, responses, and outcomes, AI can identify patterns and trends that suggest the most effective strategies for responding to similar rejections. This includes suggesting amendments to claims that not only address the examiner's concerns but also maintain the broadest possible protection for the invention, grounded in the original disclosure.[109]

One of the most innovative applications of AI in this context is its ability to analyze the behavior and tendencies of specific art units or examiners. By examining the history of an art unit or examiner's decisions, AI can guide the attorney in tailoring the response to align with the preferences or persuasions that have historically met with approval.[110] This might involve emphasizing certain arguments or citing particular kinds of precedents known to resonate with the examiner or the art unit.

Furthermore, AI can suggest amendments based on the original disclosure, providing indications of how likely these amendments are to overcome the examiner's rejections. This is not a simple keyword

---

108 Tabrez Y. Ebrahim, *Automation & Predictive Analytics in Patent Prosecution: USPTO Implication & Policy*, 35 Ga. St. U. L. Rev. 1185, 1200-1201 (2019) (AI's ability to aid is not limited to drafting but also responses to office actions).

109 *Id.*

110 Stephen Rynkiewicz, *Paralegal Robot Reviews Patent Documents*, ABA JOURNAL (Mar. 22, 2024), http://www.abajournal.com/news/article/patent_document_robot_legal_review [https://perma.cc/3SW2-566G].

match but a nuanced understanding of the technology, the law, and the specific language that has succeeded in the past. These suggestions come with an analysis of potential trade-offs, helping attorneys to make informed decisions about how to balance claim breadth with the likelihood of success.[111]

The integration of AI into patent prosecution, especially in responding to office actions, represents a leap forward in how attorneys navigate the patenting process. It offers a blend of analytical depth, strategic foresight, and efficiency that can significantly enhance the quality of patent applications and the speed with which they are granted. This AI-driven approach doesn't replace the attorney's expertise but amplifies it, merging human insight with machine intelligence to navigate the complex landscape of patent law more effectively than ever before.

Opinion Work with AI

FTOs

Integrating AI into the process of conducting FTO analysis can help patent attorneys significantly in how they provide critical advice to clients. The essence of FTO analysis lies in determining whether a product, process, or technology can be commercialized without infringing on existing intellectual property rights.[112] Traditionally, this requires exhaustive research and nuanced legal and technical analysis, areas where AI can offer transformative assistance.

AI can revolutionize the initial stages of FTO analysis by streamlining the research process. Using advanced algorithms, AI can swiftly sift

---

111 Tabrez Y. Ebrahim, *Automation & Predictive Analytics in Patent Prosecution: USPTO Implication & Policy*, 35 Ga. St. U. L. Rev. 1185, 1202-1206 (2019) (the ability of AI to analyze historical data an create predictable outcomes).

112 Tom Baker, *What is Freedom to Operate (FTO) in relation to patents and IP?*, LEXOLOGY (Oct. 21, 2019), https://www.lexology.com/library/detail.aspx?g=38c0d68a-6a95-4769-bcf1-adc805e19c58.

through millions of patent documents, legal databases, and scientific literature to identify potentially relevant patents and published applications.[113] Unlike traditional search methods, AI can analyze documents at an unprecedented scale and speed, ensuring no critical piece of prior art is overlooked. Furthermore, AI's ability to understand and interpret complex technical language allows for more precise filtering of results, focusing on documents most relevant to the client's technology.

Once potential infringements are identified, AI can assist in the nuanced analysis of these patents against the client's product or process. By employing natural language processing and machine learning, AI can compare the claims of identified patents with the technical details of the client's offering, highlighting areas of potential overlap. This capability extends beyond simple keyword matching, allowing AI to understand context, interpret claims in light of relevant precedents, and evaluate the novelty and non-obviousness of the technology in question.[114]

Perhaps one of the most groundbreaking aspects of AI in FTO analysis is its ability to provide predictive insights. By analyzing outcomes of past patent disputes and enforcement actions within similar technology domains, AI can offer probabilistic assessments of the risks associated with proceeding to market. This predictive capability enables attorneys to offer more informed strategic recommendations, advising clients not only on the legal risks but also on potential mitigation strategies, such as licensing opportunities or minor product modifications to avoid infringement.[115]

AI's integration into FTO analysis also enhances the way attorneys communicate findings and recommendations to clients. AI can

---

113　Janet Freilich, *Patent's New Salience*, 109 Va. L. Rev. 595, 611-612 (2023) (the ability of AI to search for previous relevant patents).
114　*Id.* at 614.
115　*Id.*

help distill complex legal and technical information into clear, concise reports tailored to the client's level of expertise. This can facilitate more effective decision-making, enabling clients to weigh the legal risks against business objectives confidently.

Patent Infringement Analysis

Integrating AI into patent infringement analysis work can enhance the patent attorney's assessment of potential infringements and strategize defense or enforcement actions. This task, traditionally marked by intensive document review and nuanced legal and technical analyses, stands to be revolutionized by the capabilities AI brings to the table.[116]

When embarking on an infringement analysis, a patent attorney typically needs to dissect the claims of a patent and meticulously compare them against a product or process in question. This involves a deep dive into the technical details and a nuanced understanding of patent claim interpretation.[117] AI, with its advanced algorithms and machine learning capabilities, can significantly streamline this process.

Firstly, AI can automate the initial comparison process, scanning through patent claims and the technical specifications of the accused product to identify potential overlaps. This is achieved through NLP and semantic analysis techniques, which allow the AI to understand and interpret the complex language of patent claims in the context of real-world technologies. By doing so, AI can quickly highlight areas of concern where the product might infringe on patent claims, saving attorneys countless hours of manual comparison.[118]

Beyond identifying potential overlaps, AI can further analyze the

---

116 Dhruv Saini, *Revolutionizing Patent Infringement: Role of AI in Patent Infringement Detection and Monetization*, XLSCOUT (Jan. 24, 2024), https://xlscout.ai/revolutionizing-patent-infringement-role-of-ai-in-patent-infringement-detection-and-monetization.
117 *Id.*
118 Pramod Chintalapoodi, *The Impact of AI in IP Law*, LEXOLOGY (Mar. 7, 2024), https://www.lexology.com/library/detail.aspx?g=e3232dca-4f30-4fb3-a7c8-cd58e1c63c53.

cited references in the patent and any relevant prior art to provide a comprehensive background for each claim.[119] This helps in understanding the scope of the claims and how they have been interpreted in the past, offering insights into possible defenses based on prior art or claim limitations.

Moreover, AI's data analysis capabilities come into play by assessing the likelihood of infringement based on historical data from similar cases. By analyzing outcomes of past infringement cases with comparable claim overlaps, AI can predict the potential success of an infringement claim or defense. This predictive analysis can guide attorneys in advising their clients on the feasibility of litigation, potential outcomes, and alternative strategies, such as seeking a settlement or license agreement.

AI can also offer strategic insights into the behavior of specific patent holders or competitors based on their litigation history. Understanding whether a patent holder is litigious, for instance, or if a competitor has a history of settling infringement disputes can inform the strategy for dealing with potential infringement issues.

Patent Invalidity Analysis

Integrating AI into patent invalidity analysis work can greatly enhance the way patent attorneys approach challenges to the validity of patents, whether in defense against infringement allegations or as a proactive measure to clear the path for new products. This complex and critical task, traditionally reliant on exhaustive research and nuanced legal analysis, is significantly enhanced by AI's computational power and analytical capabilities.

---

119   David Cain, *Strategic Patenting: AI-aided Patent Strategy and Competitive Intelligence,* LINKEDIN (Jan. 24, 2024), https://www.linkedin.com/pulse/ai-aided-patent-strategy-competitive-intelligence-david-cain-e8usc/?trk=article-ssr-frontend-pulse_more-articles_related-content-card.

One of the foundational elements of invalidity analysis is the identification of prior art that could potentially invalidate a patent.[120] AI excels in this domain, utilizing advanced search algorithms to sift through vast databases of patents, scientific literature, and technical publications. By processing natural language queries and understanding technical jargon, AI can uncover relevant prior art more efficiently than traditional search methods. This not only speeds up the initial discovery process but also ensures a comprehensive review that might reveal obscure but critical pieces of prior art overlooked by human researchers.[121]

After identifying potential prior art, the next step involves a detailed analysis of the patent claims in question and mapping these claims against the discovered prior art. AI tools, equipped with sophisticated pattern recognition capabilities, can automate parts of this process. They analyze the language and scope of the patent claims and compare them to the features and disclosures of the prior art, identifying areas of overlap or potential novelty issues. This aids attorneys in constructing arguments for invalidity based on detailed, claim-by-claim comparisons.

Beyond the identification and mapping of prior art, AI can provide invaluable insights into the likelihood of success in challenging a patent's validity. By analyzing historical data on patent invalidation cases, including factors that contributed to successful invalidation, AI can predict the potential outcomes of pursuing an invalidity argument. This predictive analysis helps attorneys advise their clients on the risks and benefits of pursuing invalidity challenges, optimizing legal strategies based on data-driven insights.

---

120 *Patent Invalidity Search: What Is It and How Do I Perform One?*, INQUARTIK (Mar. 26, 2020), https://www.inquartik.com/blog/basic-patent-invalidity-search/.

121 Pramod Chintalapoodi, *The Impact of AI in IP Law*, LEXOLOGY (Mar. 7, 2024), https://www.lexology.com/library/detail.aspx?g=e3232dca-4f30-4fb3-a7c8-cd58e1c63c53.

AI's analytical prowess also extends to examining the patent office's examination history of the patent in question and any related litigation. This examination can reveal procedural weaknesses or inconsistencies in the patent prosecution process that might be leveraged in an invalidity argument. Additionally, analyzing litigation histories, including how similar arguments have fared in court, provides strategic insights that inform the development of a robust invalidity case.

Finally, AI's role in patent invalidity analysis isn't limited to a one-time review. Continuous monitoring capabilities mean that AI systems can alert attorneys to new publications, patents, or legal developments that might impact ongoing invalidity analyses. This ongoing analysis ensures that attorneys and their clients can adapt their strategies in response to the evolving intellectual property landscape, maintaining a proactive stance on patent validity issues.

The integration of AI into patent invalidity analysis work transforms a traditionally labor-intensive and time-consuming process into a streamlined, data-driven operation. This evolution not only enhances the efficiency and effectiveness of invalidity challenges but also empowers patent attorneys with deeper insights, enabling more strategic, informed decision-making in the protection and enforcement of intellectual property rights.

A Week in the Life of a Patent Attorney ... with AI

Embarking on a reimagined journey through a week in the life of a patent attorney, we now explore the transformative impact of AI on their daily activities. This narrative unveils how the integration of AI tools into the core functions of patent law—searching, drafting, prosecution, and opinion work—will herald a new era of efficiency, precision, and strategic insight. Gone are the days of labor-intensive processes consuming the bulk of the workweek. Instead, we step into a world where tasks that once spanned days are now accomplished in hours, where the attorney's deep legal acumen is augmented by the speed and analytical power of AI. This week showcases not just a shift in how work is done but a revolution in what can be achieved, setting the stage for a future where patent attorneys harness AI to navigate the complex landscape of intellectual property law more effectively than ever before. As we venture into this narrative, it's important to recognize it as a forward vision—a glimpse into a near future where such synergies between patent attorneys and AI are not just speculative fiction but an impending reality. This exploration into what will most certainly be possible invites us to imagine the profound changes on the horizon, promising a leap towards unprecedented efficiency and insight into the practice of patent law.

Day One - Patent Search and Paten Drafting

Patent Search – early morning

The day begins in the early morning, with our patent attorney equipped not just with legal expertise but with the power of AI. The task of patent searching, once a day-long endeavor, is now streamlined into an efficient, precise process.

Upon arriving at the office, the attorney outlines the invention's key features in a succinct brief. This brief is then input into the AI system, which is designed to understand and process natural language descriptions of inventions. There's no need for exhaustive manual formulation of search queries; the AI does the heavy lifting, interpreting the attorney's inputs and preparing for a targeted search. Within minutes, the AI tool scans through millions of patent documents and scientific publications. Its advanced algorithms, capable of contextual understanding and semantic analysis, identify relevant prior art with a precision and depth that surpasses traditional search methods.

By the time the attorney finishes their first cup of coffee, the AI system has not only identified pertinent documents but also analyzed their relevance to the invention. It ranks these findings, highlighting potential overlaps and areas where the invention stands out. This analysis is then compiled into a concise report, ready for the attorney's review. The report includes summaries of the most relevant patents, providing a clear overview of the landscape the invention is entering.

Before the morning has barely begun, what would have previously taken a whole day is completed. The attorney reviews the AI-generated report, armed with comprehensive insights into the patent landscape. This rapid turnaround doesn't just save time; it provides a solid foundation for the next steps, now with the entire day ahead to focus on them.

With the efficiency gained from AI in patent searching, the attorney now turns their attention to patent drafting. The morning's success sets a positive tone for the day, promising a similar transformation in how the patent application will be crafted, thanks to AI assistance. The attorney is poised to tackle this next crucial phase, ready to leverage AI's capabilities to not just match but enhance the quality of work done in significantly less time.

Patent Drafting Early morning to afternoon.

By late morning, the focus shifts to drafting the patent application. Our attorney, energized by the quick wins of the early hours, begins by outlining the invention's details and claims structure in the AI-assisted drafting tool. This tool, designed to understand the intricacies of patent law and the technical nuances of the invention, uses natural language processing to translate the attorney's inputs into a preliminary draft.

The AI system suggests claims based on the invention's features and the results of the morning's patent search, ensuring that the claims are robust and encompass the invention's novelty while avoiding overlaps with existing patents. It drafts descriptions that are technically detailed and legally precise, pulling from a database of patent language that has been successful in past applications, as well as any necessary figures. This not only speeds up the drafting process but also ensures that the language used aligns with patent office expectations.

By midday, the attorney reviews the AI-generated draft, refining the language and claims with their expert judgment. AI's initial suggestions for claim amendments and specification enhancements are evaluated. The attorney leverages AI tools to simulate how different claim constructions might hold up against potential challenges, using predictive analytics based on historical patent data. This process allows the attorney to strategically strengthen the application, ensuring maximum protection for the invention.

In the early afternoon, the focus turns to ensuring the draft complies with all legal and procedural requirements. The AI system automatically checks the draft against patent office guidelines, highlighting any sections that need adjustments to meet formatting standards or other regulatory criteria. This automated review process eliminates the need for time-consuming manual checks, allowing the attorney to quickly make necessary adjustments.

At this time, the patent application draft is in its final form, thoroughly reviewed and enhanced with AI's analytical power and the attorney's legal expertise. The draft is not only technically and legally robust but also strategically positioned to navigate through the patent office's examination process efficiently.

The attorney sends the completed draft to the client for review, well ahead of schedule. This accelerated timeline, made possible by AI integration, opens up new possibilities for client engagement and strategic planning. The attorney can now spend the additional time gained on deeper consultations, further innovation strategy development, or beginning work on new projects.

The completion of the patent drafting process by the afternoon marks a significant achievement, showcasing the drastic efficiency improvements AI brings to patent law practice. What traditionally might have taken days of meticulous labor is now accomplished in a single day, without compromising quality or thoroughness. This reimagined workday not only highlights the potential of AI to transform patent drafting but also exemplifies a future where attorneys can leverage technology to amplify their impact, dedicating more time to strategic advice and innovation protection.

<u>Patent Prosecution - late afternoon.</u>

As the late afternoon of this transformative first day unfolds, our patent attorney, now significantly ahead of schedule thanks to the integration of AI in patent searching and drafting, turns their attention to patent prosecution, specifically addressing an office action. This phase, traditionally seen as a not-so-easy task due to its complexity and the meticulous attention it demands, is now re-envisioned through the lens of AI efficiency.

The office action, a critical point in the patent prosecution process, requires a detailed response to the patent office's concerns regarding the patent application. In the past, this would have involved significant time of analyzing the cited references, formulating arguments, and drafting a response. Now, armed with AI, our attorney approaches this task with a new level of efficiency.

Immediately upon receiving the office action, the attorney inputs it into the AI system, which has been finely tuned to their preferences and legal style. Within minutes, the AI analyzes the document, identifying the key issues raised by the examiner. It cross-references the cited prior art against the application in question, pinpointing exactly where the examiner's concerns lie and suggesting areas where the application can be amended or where additional arguments can be made to overcome the objections.

Leveraging the attorney's historical responses and successful strategies, the AI proposes a draft response that meticulously addresses each point raised in the office action. This draft includes suggested amendments to the claims, supported by a rationale that aligns with the attorney's style and past successes. It also highlights potential precedents and legal arguments that could further strengthen the case for patentability.

With the AI's assistance, what would have taken hours of manual effort now takes mere minutes. The attorney reviews the draft response, making any necessary adjustments to ensure that it fully captures their strategic approach and adheres to their client's goals. This review process is swift, as the AI's suggestions are closely aligned with the attorney's preferences, ensuring that the response is both comprehensive and persuasive.

By the end of the day, the attorney submits the response to the patent office, confident in its ability to address the examiner's concerns effectively. This submission, completed in a fraction of the usual time, marks a significant milestone in the patent prosecution process and showcases the dramatic impact of AI on the efficiency and effectiveness of handling office actions.

Day Two - Opinion Work

Day Two in our reimagined week with the AI-empowered patent attorney unfolds with a showcase of efficiency and strategic depth as they tackle Freedom to Operate (FTO) analysis, patent infringement analysis, and patent invalidity analysis—all within a single day. This rapid progression through tasks, traditionally spread over several days or even weeks, highlights the transformative impact of AI in the realm of intellectual property law.

The day begins with an FTO analysis, a critical step for clients considering launching new products. In this AI-enhanced workflow, the attorney inputs the product specifications and relevant technical fields into the AI system. Within moments, the AI conducts a comprehensive search through global patent databases, identifying existing patents that could potentially impede the client's product launch. The AI's capability to understand complex technical descriptions and legal nuances ensures a thorough and precise search, vastly outpacing traditional methods.

By mid-morning, the attorney reviews the AI-generated report, which not only lists potentially conflicting patents but also provides an initial assessment of the risk posed by each. This rapid turnaround allows the attorney to quickly move on to in-depth analysis, focusing their expertise on evaluating the legal implications and strategizing next steps for mitigating any identified risks.

Transitioning seamlessly to patent infringement analysis, the attorney leverages AI to examine a competitor's product that may infringe upon the client's patent. The AI system analyzes the competitor's product details against the client's patent claims, utilizing advanced algorithms to identify potential infringements. This process, enriched by AI's capacity for detailed comparison and historical data analysis, provides a nuanced understanding of the infringement landscape.

The attorney, armed with the AI's insights, develops a strategic approach for addressing the infringement. By early afternoon, they have not only assessed the infringement risk but also outlined a potential course of legal action or negotiation, ready to advise the client with data-backed recommendations.

The final task of the day, patent invalidity analysis, is approached with the same AI-driven efficiency. The attorney sets the AI to work on analyzing the validity of a competitor's patent, which the client aims to challenge. The AI sifts through prior art, patent databases, and legal precedents, identifying vulnerabilities in the patent's claims and potential grounds for invalidity.

With the AI's comprehensive analysis in hand, the attorney evaluates the strength of an invalidity claim against the competitor's patent. By late afternoon, they have synthesized the AI's findings into a strategic plan for challenging the patent, including drafting initial arguments for invalidity based on solid evidence and legal precedent.

As Day Two comes to a close, the attorney reflects on the monumental tasks accomplished in just one day—FTO analysis, patent infringement analysis, and patent invalidity analysis, each completed with the depth and thoroughness that AI-enhanced processes allow. The efficiency gained frees up time for strategic client consultations, offering insights and planning next steps in their intellectual property journey.

Week's End

As our reimagined week comes to a close—remarkably, at the end of Day Two—it's hard not to picture our patent attorney, who has just compressed a week's worth of meticulous legal work into two hyper-efficient days, gleefully eyeing their golf clubs for an unexpected midweek outing. Indeed, the mental image of the attorney swapping legal briefs for golf tees, thanks to AI's prowess, offers a light-hearted glimpse into the newfound flexibility in their schedule.

Yet, beyond the humor and the allure of a leisurely round of golf lies a deeper and more impactful reality. The efficiency unlocked by AI doesn't just open up opportunities for personal time; it fundamentally enhances the attorney's capacity to serve their clients. With the heavy lifting of research, analysis, and drafting significantly streamlined, the attorney can now allocate more time to strategic thinking, client consultation, and personalized service.

This newfound efficiency means that our attorney can take on a broader array of cases, extending their expertise to a larger number of clients who can benefit from their specialized skills. It also allows for deeper dives into complex legal challenges, where the nuances of strategy and the subtleties of argumentation can make all the difference. Furthermore, this shift can lead to innovation within the practice itself, as the attorney explores new services, delves into emerging areas of patent law, or even develops AI-driven tools tailored to their clients' specific needs.

Moreover, this transformation has implications beyond the individual attorney's practice. It heralds a shift in the legal profession towards greater accessibility and responsiveness, as more work can be done in less time, reducing wait times and potentially even costs for clients. This not only enhances the value proposition of legal services but also contributes to a more dynamic and innovative intellectual property ecosystem.

In essence, while the prospect of more frequent golf games might be an amusing side effect of AI integration, the true significance lies in the profound impact on the attorney's professional life and the broader legal landscape. The integration of AI into patent law practice represents a leap forward in how legal services are delivered, promising a future where attorneys can do more, do it better, and do it with an eye towards the evolving needs of their clients in the fast-paced world of innovation.

Our Patent Attorney Does not fear AI.

As we stand on the precipice of this new era, where AI intertwines with the practice of patent law, it's essential to view AI not as a harbinger of obsolescence for legal professionals, but as a tool that elevates and expands their capabilities. Much like the advent of the car revolutionized human mobility, transforming our capacity to explore and connect, AI serves to enhance our intellectual and professional horizons. The apprehension that AI might replace human roles misses the broader perspective—AI is a tool, a sword in the hands of those skilled enough to wield it. In the right hands, it becomes an extension of our capabilities, not a replacement. It can cut through the mundane and the cumbersome, allowing legal practitioners to focus on the essence of their craft: strategic thinking, creativity, and human judgment. Thus, rather than yielding to fear, embracing AI is about harnessing its power to become better, more efficient, and more effective in our roles, transforming challenges into opportunities and setting new standards of excellence in the legal profession.

This expansion of capabilities through AI doesn't merely optimize existing processes; it opens doors to new realms of possibility. With AI, patent attorneys can explore more innovative solutions, undertake broader analyses, and provide richer, more nuanced advice to their clients. The technology empowers them to go beyond traditional boundaries, enabling a deeper dive into the implications of patent law and its application in an ever-evolving technological landscape. It encourages a forward-thinking approach, where attorneys can anticipate future trends and prepare their clients not just for the market today but for the innovations of tomorrow.

Moreover, the integration of AI into patent law signifies a shift towards a more collaborative approach to problem-solving. AI doesn't replace the human element; it enhances it, fostering a synergy between human insight and machine efficiency. This collaboration is key to navigating the complexities of patent law, where the subtleties of language, the intricacies of technical invention, and the nuances of legal interpretation require a sophisticated, multi-faceted approach.

In embracing AI, patent attorneys are not ceding their ground but broadening their horizons. They are positioning themselves at the forefront of a new paradigm in legal practice, one that values adaptability, efficiency, and a deep commitment to leveraging the best tools available for the benefit of their clients. This era of AI in patent law is not a challenge to the profession but a testament to its evolution, a clear signal that the future of legal practice is one of enhanced capability, expanded possibility, and elevated standards of excellence.

5

So, what of AI and the Patent Attorney?

In this chapter, we delve into the varied and significant implications stemming from the integration of AI into the patent attorney's practice. While our exploration aims to shed light on key aspects, it's important to acknowledge that this overview is far from exhaustive. The transformative nature of AI in this field is vast and multifaceted, opening up a spectrum of potential effects and considerations that extend beyond the scope of our discussion. As such, there may well be implications that we haven't touched upon, and you, the reader, may envision additional impacts that escaped our consideration. The crucial takeaway is the undeniable fact that AI's integration into patent law is set to bring about profound changes. Its transformative potential is not merely hypothetical but a tangible shift that will redefine the contours of patent practice.

Increased Efficiency and Quality

The integration of AI into the patent attorney's toolkit heralds a significant leap in both efficiency and quality across various facets of their practice, notably in patent research, drafting, and prosecution. By leveraging AI tools, patent attorneys can expect a transformative shift in how they approach their work, addressing critical questions about the role of technology in enhancing their capabilities.

AI's capability to process and analyze vast datasets at speeds no human could match significantly enhances the efficiency of patent research. This includes identifying prior art more effectively than traditional search methods. AI algorithms, designed to understand and interpret complex technical language, can sift through global patent databases, scientific journals, and other technical publications to identify relevant prior art with unparalleled precision. This not only accelerates the research process but also reduces the risk of missing critical documents, thereby increasing the thoroughness of the patentability assessment.

However, the reliance on AI for patent research introduces considerations about potential oversights. While AI can drastically reduce the chances of missing relevant prior art, the nuances of human judgment are crucial in evaluating the relevance and impact of identified documents. The risk lies not in the capability of AI to identify documents but in ensuring that the legal and technical implications are accurately interpreted and applied to each unique case.

In patent drafting, AI tools can offer substantial improvements in the quality of patent applications. AI-driven drafting assistance can help in formulating clear, concise, and comprehensive patent claims and descriptions. By analyzing a vast array of granted patents and utilizing machine learning to understand what constitutes a successful patent claim, AI can guide attorneys in crafting applications that are not only legally robust but also more likely to withstand the scrutiny of patent examiners and potential legal challenges.

This approach to drafting with AI assistance ensures that every application benefits from insights derived from a broad spectrum of patent literature, potentially elevating the quality of the draft beyond what is achievable through traditional methods alone. However, the attorney's role in supervising and refining the output of AI tools is paramount to ensure that the final application accurately reflects the invention and aligns with strategic objectives.

The prosecution phase stands to gain significantly from AI integration, particularly in responding to office actions and interacting with patent offices. AI can predict the likelihood of different prosecution outcomes based on historical data, suggest strategies for overcoming rejections, and even automate routine correspondence. This not only speeds up the prosecution process but also allows attorneys to allocate more time to complex negotiations or strategy development.

While AI offers a promising avenue to increase efficiency and quality in patent prosecution, it is vital to remain vigilant about the nuances of human interaction and negotiation with patent examiners. AI can guide and inform these processes, but the attorney's expertise in navigating the subtleties of legal argumentation and examiner preferences remains irreplaceable.

The integration of AI into the practice of patent attorneys undeniably brings about increased efficiency and potential quality improvements across research, drafting, and prosecution. The evolution of AI tools promises a future where patent attorneys can achieve more in less time while elevating the standard of their work. However, this technological advancement does not diminish the need for skilled human judgment but rather enhances the attorney's ability to apply their expertise more effectively and strategically.

Client Expectations amid AI Technology

As clients become more tech-savvy, there may be an increasing expectation for attorneys to leverage AI tools, which in turn provides more efficient and effective legal services. However, while clients may appreciate the benefits of AI, there also needs to be a distinction between the insight and creativity that AI can bring to the table, and the insight and creativity that a human attorney can bring to the table. Clients will more than likely value the insight and the judgment that human attorneys bring. For this reason, it is advisable that clients and attorneys set clear rules and expectations of what their relationship will be like, and what percentage of work, if any, can be completed and generated by AI. Alongside this, it should be left clear that all work created by the help of AI will be revised by an attorney before any sort of submission, and should advise that while AI can be used as a tool for their case, it will be only to enhance their expertise, and not replace it.[122]

Further, as mentioned before, AI tools can increase efficiency, which means that they will probably reduce the time and cost associated with legal tasks. Attorneys should be clear and transparent about how AI was used in their case and regarding the fees that entail using AI as a tool. Transparent communication about these cost structures can help build trust and manage client expectations. This in turn will create more transparency and trust amongst the attorney and the client. Of course, following all ethical rules set forth in the legal field, incorporating the help of AI should be simple and beneficial to all parties. Finally, there will be times where a client does not feel comfortable with an attorney using AI in their case. Attorneys should be adaptable to client preferences regarding the use of AI, if at all possible.

However, clients may be wary of the risks posed by the early integration of AI. AI-based tools require vast amounts of data to function properly, and therefore the data that is required must not only be correct but also complete. If the data provided to the system is incorrect or

---

122 John Villasenor, *How AI will revolutionize the practice of law*, THE BROOKINGS INSTITUTION (Mar. 20, 2023), https://www.brookings.edu/articles/how-ai-will-revolutionize-the-practice-of-law/.

otherwise incomplete it might produce inaccurate results or else those inaccuracies can lead to potential infringement.[123] There are already stories of lawyers who have blindly relied upon AI tools to their client's and their detriment.[124] Another potential risk lies within the bias of the data. If the algorithms within the system are not programmed properly it can lead to biases within the drafting process. It is essential that the algorithms are designed to prioritize both accuracy and fairness over other factors such as speed and cost effectiveness.[125]

Another significant consideration that will undoubtedly impact clients' view of the adoption of AI-based tools deals with oversights. To explore this, we ask the following questions: in the event of an error, oversight, or missed prior art, who bears the responsibility? The AI developers? The law firm that used the AI-based tool? The patent attorney?

Currently in our legal framework, AI systems lack the capacity of legal agency and moral responsibility. The creates a challenge when an AI based outcome, let to negative results. To this day, legal and moral responsibility remains tied to the attorney present. Therefore, the attorneys bear the responsibility of the choices made based on the outputs of the AI tool. This is why investing in education for attorneys in AI systems is crucial in today's age. By understanding the potential risks and limitations of AI, attorneys are capable of understanding when and how to use AI as a tool for the benefit of the client. Understanding the systems can help prevent issues that might arise and mitigate the negative consequences of AI outputs.[126]

---

123 *Id.*
124 Sara Merken, *New York lawyers sanctioned for using fake ChatGPT cases in legal brief*, REUTERS (Jun. 26, 2023), https://www.reuters.com/legal/new-york-lawyers-sanctioned-using-fake-chatgpt-cases-legal-brief-2023-06-22/.
125 *Id.*
126 Maurice Bretzfield, *Responsibility and Accountability in Generative AI for Legal Applications: Navigating Ethical Challenges*, LINKEDIN (Oct. 11, 2023), https://www.linkedin.com/pulse/

Yet attorneys are not strictly liable for the AI's shortcomings. AI developers and operators can be held liable for breaches of their contractual terms, such as protection of clients' data.[127] That is why lawyers should reduce uncertainties on liabilities with contractual provisions until a standard of care relating to AI systems is established by the courts or by the governing body. Provisions such as warranties and indemnities for AI products can allocate liability in a way that firm or attorney can be protected until a clear standard is established.[128]

It is clear that transparency and trust in the attorney-client relationship will be crucial as AI becomes more prevalent in legal practice. Attorneys should actively communicate with clients, explaining the role of AI in their practice, managing expectations, and ensuring that ethical considerations are forefront in the use of these technologies. Balancing the benefits of AI with transparent communication and human oversight can contribute to a positive and trusting attorney-client relationship in the age of AI.

Some Ethical Considerations

Many ethical considerations arise with the use of AI tools. An interesting question we ask to explore some of those ethical consideration is as follows: if AI assists or even autonomously drafts certain sections of a patent, how does this impact the attorney's duty of competence?

The ABA Model Rules state, "A lawyer shall provide competent representation to a client. Competent representation requires the legal knowledge, skill, thoroughness, and preparation reasonably necessary

---

responsibility-accountability-generative-ai-legal-maurice-bretzfield/.

127 Luka Đurić & Janko Ignjatović, *Who's Responsible? Addressing Liability in the Age of AI*, GECIĆ LAW (Jun. 22, 2023), https://geciclaw.com/whos-responsible-addressing-liability-in-the-age-of-artificial-intelligence/.

128 William A. Tanenbaum, Kiyong Song & Linda A. Malek, *Theories of AI liability: It's still about the human element*, REUTERS (Sep. 20, 2022), https://www.reuters.com/legal/litigation/theories-ai-liability-its-still-about-human-element-2022-09-20/.

for the representation."[129] A lawyer's duty of competence at the end of the day is nondelegable to a nonlawyer. While a lawyer may rely on the outcome of an AI tool, the lawyer must vet any output from such tools. Failure to do so can fail to meet the duty of competence air AI tools are a starting point never an end product the professional obligations that lawyers have requires them to thoroughly review any work product that is AI generated to ensure accuracy. [130] Although the duty of competence is nondelegable nonlawyers, the attorney may rely on advisors with establish technical competence in the field at hand.[131]

Something else to consider, which may become an issue shortly, is the lack of use of AI tools and other technologies. The ABA states in the comments of Rule 1.1 that a lawyer should keep abreast of changes in the law and its practice, including the benefits and risks associated with relevant technology to maintain their competence. With new advances, the rules must always be revised in order to protect the clients.[132]

Another question we might ask is as follows: can an attorney ethically rely on AI's suggestions without a deep understanding of the underlying algorithms?

As stated above, the ABA requires awareness of the benefits and risks associated with relevant technology, but this does not simply mean being aware of the tools and whether they should be used or not. The ABA also requires an understanding of the tool, to meet the duty of competence. Here for the duty of competence to be met, the lawyer must understand not only the system itself but the data that was

---

129 MODEL RULES OF PRO. CONDUCT r. 1.1 (AM. BAR ASS'N 1983).

130 Brad Hise & Jenny Dao, *Ethical considerations in the use of AI*, REUTERS (Oct. 2, 2023), https://www.reuters.com/legal/legalindustry/ethical-considerations-use-ai-2023-10-02/.

131 Daniel W. Linna Jr. & Wendy J. Muchman, *Ethical Obligations to Protect Client Data when Building Artificial Intelligence Tools: Wigmore Meets AI*, AMERICAN BAR ASSOCIATION (Oct. 2, 2020), https://www.americanbar.org/groups/professional_responsibility/publications/professional_lawyer/27/1/ethical-obligations-protect-client-data-when-building-artificial-intelligence-tools-wigmore-meets-ai/.

132 *Id.*

used in order to create results. As well they need to determine if the tool would aid in the matter. Lastly, attorneys at times may be required to consult with technology experts in order to understand the tools they are using and how the tool can be properly implemented in the manner.[133]

Privacy and Confidentiality of Data

The application of artificial intelligence (AI) is radically transforming the way patents are developed and processed. However, its use raises considerable questions around privacy and confidentiality.

The ABA Model Rules state that "(a) a lawyer shall not reveal information relating to the representation of a client unless the client gives informed consent, the disclosure is impliedly authorized to carry out the representation, or the disclosure is permitted by paragraph (b)," and that, "A lawyer shall make reasonable efforts to prevent the inadvertent or unauthorized disclosure of, or unauthorized access to, information relating to the representation of a client."[134] Confidentiality is one of the most important rules that lawyers must abide by. Breaches in confidentiality could negatively affect your client's case. Hence it is important to make sure that all tools used by lawyers treat sensitive client data with the utmost level of confidentiality.

In order to create results, AI tools use prompts, which are queries that are inputted to generate results within the AI system. The issue is that at times these prompts are used by AI tools to improve their models and systems. This is why it's important to understand the system a lawyer is using, because if not there might be a breach of confidentiality that the lawyer is not even aware of. That is not all, some AI tools hire third party contractors to review how the system is functioning;

---

133 *Id.*
134 MODEL RULES OF PRO. CONDUCT r. 1.6 (AM. BAR ASS'N 1983).

reviewing both input and output. This means that inputting confidential data to the queries could result in a breach of confidentiality if the data is being exposed to outside parties. [135]

When contracting an expert or vendor, the responsibility still belongs to the attorney, and the final product still has to be revised by them. If a third party is involved in the development of a tool, the attorney or firm's duty to supervise nonlawyers is implicated. If a tool is created by a third party, or when a third-party's cloud software is used to store data needed for the AI tool, the lawyers must take steps to fulfill their duties of confidentiality to their clients. The reasonable expectation of confidentiality in these situations includes ensuring that the third-party provider, like the attorney, has an enforceable obligation of confidentiality as well as the requirement to notify the attorney or firm of any disclosures of clients' information. The attorney must also make sure to investigate the provider's security of their system to ensure that they are adequate. As well, there must be a commitment to employing technology to prevent any foreseeable attempts to access unauthorized client data and lastly, for the attorney to confirm the third party's ability to "purge and wipe" the clients' data. [136]

Therefore, when outsourcing the development of an AI tool to a third party, the lawyer or firm should ensure that the third party has an enforceable obligation to protect the confidentiality and security of any data belonging to the clients. The agreement should also include language that limits the use of client information by the third party

---

135 Shabbi S. Khan & Kathleen E. Wegrzyn, *IP Lawyer vs. ChatGPT: Top 10 Legal Issues of Using Generative AI at Work*, FOLEY (Mar. 27, 2023), https://www.foley.com/insights/publications/2023/03/ip-lawyer-vs-chatgpt-top-10-legal-issues-ai-work/.

136 Daniel W. Linna Jr. & Wendy J. Muchman, *Ethical Obligations to Protect Client Data when Building Artificial Intelligence Tools: Wigmore Meets AI*, AMERICAN BAR ASSOCIATION (Oct. 2, 2020), https://www.americanbar.org/groups/professional_responsibility/publications/professional_lawyer/27/1/ethical-obligations-protect-client-data-when-building-artificial-intelligence-tools-wigmore-meets-ai/.

except for as agreed upon. As well the agreement should obligate the third party to take adequate protections to ensure the safety of the data from online theft.[137]

AI and Safeguarding Data Confidentiality.

There can be no question, especially when using AI-based tools, it is critical to ensure that this information remains confidential.

One strategy to achieve this is to employ anonymization and pseudonymization techniques. These tactics can help to safeguard the identity of patent applicants and the specific nature of their inventions. However, it is important to note that these techniques are not fool-proof and must be complemented by other security measures.

Artificial Intelligence (AI) systems play a crucial role in a number of areas, and their effectiveness often depends on the use of extensive amounts of data. In the context of patents in Mexico, this data can include highly confidential information linked to patented inventions and technologies. Ensuring the confidentiality of this information becomes imperative to safeguard the interests of applicants and the innovation ecosystem in general.

Anonymization and pseudonymization are techniques used to safeguard confidential data in patents and other documents related to artificial intelligence (AI), as mentioned above. These practices seek to protect the privacy and sensitive information of individuals or companies involved in the development of patented technologies. But we would like to give a detailed description of both techniques: [138]

---

137 *Id.*
138 Leticia Garcia-Blanch Sanz de Andino, *Diferencia entre anonimizacion y pseudonimizacion de datos personales: un analisis tecnico-juridico*, ECONOMIST&JURIST (Aug. 24, 2022), https://www.economistjurist.es/articulos-juridicos-destacados/diferencia-entre-anonimizacion-y-pseudonimi-zacion-de-datos-personales-un-analisis-tecnico-juridico/.

1) Anonymization:

Anonymization is a process by which certain details of a data set are removed or modified to make it impossible or very difficult to associate the information with specific individuals.27

— In the context of AI-assisted patents, anonymization may involve the removal of names, addresses, identification numbers and any other information that can identify the parties involved.

— Removal of Personally Identifiable Information (PII): Information that can identify a person, such as names, addresses, telephone numbers, etc., is removed from the patent document.

— Reduction of Specific Details: Specific details that could be linked to a particular entity can be reduced or generalized. For example, instead of providing precise details about the location of a company, the region or country could be mentioned.

— Modification of Dates and Quantities: Specific dates and quantities can also be modified to avoid direct identification of events or transactions.

— De-identification of Images and Graphics: If patents contain images or graphics that reveal sensitive information, they can be de-identified or modified to ensure anonymity.

2) Pseudonymization:

Pseudonymization involves replacing identifying data with fictitious identifiers or pseudonyms. Although the data is altered, it is still possible to associate the information with a specific individual using a certain key or additional information.

— Use of Fictitious Identifiers: Names, identification

numbers, or other identifying information are replaced with fictitious identifiers or pseudonyms.

- Pseudonymization Keys: A key or additional information is used to link the pseudonym to the real identity when necessary. This key is kept securely and is only available to those with specific permissions.139

Pseudonymization Key Protection: The key used to reverse pseudonymization is securely maintained and only shared with authorized personnel. This helps ensure that the information can be retrieved only by those who have the need and right to access it.

Both techniques, anonymization and pseudonymization, are essential to ensure privacy protection and data security in artificial intelligence-related patents. However, it is important to keep in mind that no method is completely foolproof, and security practices must be continually evaluated and updated to adapt to constantly evolving threats.

Now, we have already noted that anonymization seeks to remove or modify data that could reveal the identity of the parties involved, while pseudonymization involves replacing identifying data with artificial information. These tactics, when properly applied, contribute significantly to the protection of sensitive data.

In addition to anonymization and pseudonymization, other security measures are available that can strengthen the confidentiality of patent applications. These include the use of encryption to protect data during transit or storage, as well as the implementation of access controls to restrict who can access such information.

Encryption and access controls are critical components for

---

139 *Anonimiacion y seudonimizacion de datos personales: caracteristicas y diferencias*, NORMADAT (Nov. 30, 2022), https://www.normadat.es/anonimizacion-y-seudonimizacion-de-datos-personales-caracteristicas-y-diferencias/.

safeguarding sensitive data in artificial intelligence (AI)-related patents. These measures help protect the integrity, confidentiality and availability of information. Here it would be pertinent to explain and detail how encryption and access controls are applied in this context:

1) Encryption:
   a. Encryption is the process of scrambling information so that only those authorized can access it. In the context of AI patents, encryption can be applied at the file, database or communication level.[140]
2) Access Controls:
   a. Access controls define who is allowed to access what resources and under what conditions. To protect sensitive data in AI patents, various access controls are implemented.[141]

It is crucial to keep in mind that, despite the effectiveness of anonymization and pseudonymization techniques, it should be stressed that they are not infallible on their own. In the context of AI and sensitive data management, these strategies must be complemented by other security measures. Implementing access controls, robust encryption and strong information security policies becomes a necessity to strengthen data protection and prevent potential security breaches.

In summary, bias and fairness in AI models are issues that cannot be overlooked in patent prosecution. The potential impact of biased decisions in this area not only affects individual inventors, but also has broader implications for innovation and progress. Addressing these challenges will require active collaboration between the scientific

---

140 *Como funciona la encriptacion: Todo lo que necesita saber*, GOANYWHERE (Jan. 22, 2021), https://www.goanywhere.com/es/blog/como-funciona-la-encriptacion-todo-necesita-saber.
141 *What is Access Control?*, MICROSOFT, https://www.microsoft.com/en-us/security/business/security-101/what-is-access-control.

community, AI developers, patent authorities and other relevant stakeholders to ensure a more equitable, transparent and ethical system of intellectual property protection.

AI Education in Law School and Legal Education

The education field has not been an exception to the increasing AI innovation. Students from all over the world have begun using AI powered tools in their assignments and studies. While AI is certainly an invaluable tool to enhance education, it can also hinder authenticity, accuracy, and can create multiple issues pertaining to student success and honesty.[142] A balance is required to maximize the benefits of the educational use of AI and minimize the hindrance of effects AI can have in legal education. If taught correctly and thoroughly, AI education will lead to well versed attorneys who will be more efficient and prepared to overcome legal and professional issues.

Reformulating Education

AI has revolutionized the legal field and legal education by introducing innovative tools that enhance the learning experience for students. With the growth of AI, law school educators are incorporating AI-powered tools to increase the learning experience and catering to different learning styles and student needs. One of the biggest benefits that incorporating AI to legal education brings is AI facilitating and making the extensive process of legal research more efficient for students, which in turn makes the issue of time-consuming information gathering lessen and allows for increased focus on legal analysis. What was once a grueling process of shifting through case law, statutes,

---

142 Cohen, Olivia, *ChatGPT on Campus: Law Schools Wrestle With Emerging AI Tools*,
BLOOMBERG LAW (Aug. 11, 2023), https://news.bloomberglaw.com/business-and-practice/
chatgpt-on-campus-law-schools-wrestle-with-emerging-ai-tools.

and precedents is now a simple and efficient process based on Natural Language Processing (NLP), which generates concise summaries, identifies issues, and facilitates quicker understanding of complex legal concepts. This allows students more time to focus on learning issues of the law and not on searching for the correct caselaw or statute. Further, it would provide students with correct summaries of law that can avoid misreading or misquoting the law. Not only can NLP aid in all legal precedent, but can also provide possible outcomes of legal cases based on the precedent of the law. This in turn would allow students to view probabilities in laws that are currently being tried and aid in creating arguments and promote discussion pertaining the projected results. The integration of AI education is essential for student and professional growth, and as Professor Polk Wager of the University of Pennsylvania Carley Law School, it is truly a fool's game to ban the use of AI in its entirety and rather needs to be something students become fluent in.[143] Statements such as Professor Polk Wager should be seen as proof of the legal and professional field revolutionizing to a more precise and efficient future for the legal industry.

Innovative Educational Powerhouses

Though the use of AI can go against the traditional notions of legal research, writing and education, many schools have taken it upon themselves to educate their faculty, staff and student bodies about the power of AI. Harvard Law School and Berkman Klein Center recently announced their initiative on Artificial Intelligence and the Law.[144] The initiative focuses on opportunities created by AI, such as its potential enhancements, speed of legal practice and its aid to effectiveness for

---

143 *Id.*
144 *Harvard Law School and Berkman Klein Center announce new initiative on Artificial Intelligence and the Law,* HARVARD LAW TODAY (Jul. 17, 2023), https://hls.harvard.edu/today/harvard-law-school-and-berkman-klein-center-announce-new-initiative-on-artificial-intelligence-and-the-law/.

enforcement and adjudication, and also mentions its pitfalls, such as societal issues created by AI and consumer protection, false advertising, privacy, misinformation and discrimination.[145] The addition to legal curriculum within these educational institutions not only better equip their students with knowledge of matters that are increasingly present in the legal world today, but it also demonstrates the need to move forward with the changing tools to better the individuals practicing law and the legal field.

Continuing Legal Education (CLE) and training beyond law school

Just as law students and legal education, it is essential for patent attorneys to be part of training to leverage AI tools as they have become more and more integrated into the legal practice. Patent attorneys need to make sure that they understand and have experience with the growing AI tools available by being familiar with AI processing, its capabilities, limitations, and data analytics. Understanding these tools will lead to an easier integration of hands-on experience and in turn will create numerous benefits for the attorneys and their firms and clients. AI training can help attorneys become more efficient by getting assistance in drafting patent applications and developing effective prosecution strategies. These trainings will also go hand in hand with the continuous requirement of staying updated with the most recent laws and regulations as well as more beneficial ways to help clients, such as the Model Rules in the ABA.[146]

Further, just as previously mentioned, attorneys who are being trained with these new and innovative AI tools need to keep the ethical

---

145 *Id.*
146 *See* MODEL RULES OF PRO. CONDUCT r. 1.1 cmt. 8 "To maintain the requisite knowledge and skill, a lawyer should keep abreast of changes in the law and its practice, including the benefits and risks associated with relevant technology…"

and legal considerations that utilizing AI entails. Data privacy and security need to be kept in the priority of using AI tools, especially whist using client confidential and sensitive information. Additionally, biases integrated in AI algorithms should be noted to ensure fair and accurate outcomes for them and their clients. By incorporating training programs, patent attorneys can navigate the integration of AI tools into patent practice effectively and they can ensure the benefits of these technologies while upholding ethical standards and delivering high-quality legal services to their clients.

Downfalls and Ethical Implications of AI in Legal Education

Despite the numerous benefits that AI can have in legal education, it is important that legal educators, as well as students, understand the ethical and societal implications of integrating AI to legal education. As many current law schools are doing, it is important to educate and train law students on the ethical and societal issues that AI can bring, such as issues pertaining to data privacy and protection, biases in algorithms, and how to responsibly use AI tools. This becomes especially important when students and/or attorneys use AI in order to draft or create assignments or pleadings. Not only does this possibly create issues because, as mentioned, AI can have biases, but AI technology can make mistakes. With new AI technology advancing rapidly, it leaves some tools to detect AI created documents or pleadings unable to detect if an AI tool was used. Even advanced websites or technologies can sometimes not detect generative AI tools because their evolutions are becoming too sophisticated. Further, it is important to note that AI can easily become a tool which can lead legal professionals to over-rely on. As previously mentioned, AI should be used as a tool and not as a replacement.

Some International Implications

AI has made a broad impact across the globe with each country creating its own laws and regulations pertaining to the use of AI. Though met with some speculation, most countries have adopted AI in their professional, governmental, and educational sectors. In 2023, the International Legal Generative AI Survey surveyed lawyers, law students and consumers across the U.S., U.K., Canada, and France about their overall awareness, anticipated impact and use of generative AI, and expectations of adoption.[147] From the surveyed individuals, 47% believed generative AI will have a significant and transformative impact on the practice of law; 45% of respondents believe generative AI will have some impact, while only about 7% believe generative AI will have no impact.[148]Additionally, the overall expectation among corporate counsel that law from will adopt AI technology increases to 60% agreeing that they expect law firms to adopt AI and only 10% disagreeing, Further 52% of law firms affirm that their corporate counsel client will expect them to use AI tools, and only 17% disagreeing.[149] From these countries, 67% of U.S. counsel, 61% French counsel, 59% U.K. counsel, and 53% Canadian counsel expect their law firms to adopt generative AI tools.[150]From these studies, it seems that the use of AI is favorable and that different modern countries and jurisdictions are embracing the use of AI in the legal field.

With the heightened desire and foresight of AI being part of daily patent law, multiple questions arise as to what jurisdictions will do pertaining to AI-generated inventions and what would be the threshold

---

147 *LexisNexis International Legal Generative AI Survey Shows Nearly Half of the Legal Profession Believe Generative AI Will Transform the Practice of Law*, LEXISNEXIS (Aug. 22, 2023), https://www.lexisnexis.com/community/pressroom/b/news/posts/lexisnexis-international-legal-generative-ai-survey-shows-nearly-half-of-the-legal-profession-believe-generative-ai-will-transform-the-practice-of-law.

148 *Id.*

149 *Id.*

150 *Id.*

that each jurisdiction holds when considering and granting patents. "Invention" under 35 US Code, Section 100 is defined as an "invention of discovery".[151] Under European law, the European Patent Convention (EPC) gave a negative definition of invention as a "subject matter excluded from patentability".[152] The Japanese Patent Act (JPA) defines an invention as the "highly skilled advanced creating of technical ideas utilizing the laws of nature."[153]All of these definitions from different nations and jurisdictions are broad enough to consider both AI and human generated inventions alike, however, some of these countries can be less flexible than others in the interpretation of AI generated inventions. U.S. Courts have determined that "laws of nature, physical phenomena and abstract ideas" are not patentable.[154] The laws set forth in the European Union require an invention to be concrete and have technical character that involves a technical teaching in order to solve a technical problem.[155] Under Japanese law, the use of 'laws of nature' can be interpreted as something that "embodies the principle of cause and effect that is usually inherent to a natural phenomenon".[156]Despite the fact that the three jurisdictions presented above do seem to embrace the use of AI generated inventions, it is clear that each of them can vary from flexibility from each other. Varying degrees on who is to be considered a 'skilled person in the art' and what is considered an inventive step are seen in each of the jurisdictions. These remaining differences within the jurisdictions can lead to

---

151 35 U.S.C. § 100

152 EPC Article 52(2), (3)

153 JPA Art. 2(1)

154 Diamond v. Chakrabarty, 447 U.S. 303, 309 (1980).

155 Ana Ramalho, *Patentability of AI-generated inventions: is a reform of the patent system needed?* INSTITUTE OF INTELLECTUAL PROPERTY, FOUNDATION FOR INTELLECTUAL PROPERTY OF JAPAN (Feb. 15, 2018), Referencing D. VISSER, The annotated European Patent Convention [2000], 25th ed., Kluwer Law International, 2017.

156 Ana Ramalho, *Patentability of AI-generated inventions: is a reform of the patent system needed?* INSTITUTE OF INTELLECTUAL PROPERTY, FOUNDATION FOR INTELLECTUAL PROPERTY OF JAPAN (Feb. 15, 2018).

different results in each of the jurisdictions and the inability to have reciprocity among countries, which in turn, creates strain and global implications.

The global implications that AI in patent law brings create a heightened need for harmonization of patent laws across jurisdictions and countries. The influence that AI has on patent laws has led to amendments and calcifications on them. Additional laws change on patent law can be predicted to be made in inventorship issues, the criteria for AI-related patents, and the protection of AI-generated innovations.[157]Countries will more than likely also develop new IP protocols that outline ownership and rights for AI-generated content. For these types of creating, cohesive legal frameworks need to be created to provide clear guidelines, ensuring both creators and users are being treated fairly. Additionally, all of the frameworks and creation of laws should aim to be made with a global cooperation creating the regulations of AI technologies and intellectual property. This would create a cross-border AI ecosystem that would simplify and avoid issues on a global scale.

Inconstancies in legal frameworks and definitions can lead to multiple challenges in enforcing patents, which in turn can hinder international collaborations and create barriers to the global exchange of AI related technologies. The streamlining of AI technologies is crucial in helping alleviate those challenges and create a more cohesive approach to AI related inventions. Additionally, as with all of the new and emerging technologies, the probability of cyber-attacks increases.[158] Alongside AI and patent law changes and modifications, there should

---

157 *Artificial Intelligence and IP: Where Technology Meets,* TTCONSULTANTS (Nov. 7, 2023), https://ttconsultants.com/artificial-intelligence-and-ip-where-technology-meets-law/#:~:text=Harmonizing%20AI%2Drelated%20IP%20laws,the%20cross%2Dborder%20AI%20ecosystem.&text=As%20AI%20models%20and%20data,and%20protect%20proprietary%20AI%20algorithms.

158 *Id.*

be an importance in strengthening cybersecurity. These regulations should aim at preventing IP theft and protect propriety AI algorithms.

The increase and need in harmonization of policy and law pertaining to AI and the legal field has been a part of the World Intellectual Property Organization (WIPO). In the third session of the WIPO Conversation on Intellectual Property (IP) and Artificial Intelligence (AI), which took place on January 8, 2021, a total of 133 countries attended the session pertaining to AI and its impact on daily lives worldwide.[159] Further, according to the 2019 WIPO Technology Trends on Artificial Intelligence, over 340,000 AI-related applications were received by IP addresses.[160] Among these statements, there was a census on the floor of the session that there needs to be a basic cohesive definition of AI and AI-related terms, however, it was noted that because AI technologies are rapidly-evolving, it would prove to be difficult. Similarly, issues relating to the definition of AI-generated inventions without any type of human intervention were also discussed, and as previously mentioned, presented as an issue for the global community. It is clear that strides to a more cohesive definition that would eradicate these global implications are taking place and that some sort of guidelines are being presented for adoption.

Economic Implications

Most firms are using some sort of AI or assessing technology in their everyday transactions with customers. In fact, the bast majority of the UK's top 100 law firms have reported to use some sort of AI.[161] These

---

159 WIPO Conversation on Intellectual Property (IP) and Artificial Intelligence (AI), Third Session, Geneva (Nov. 4, 2020).
160 *WIPO Technology Trends 2019: Artificial Intelligence. Geneva: World Intellectual Property Organization,* WIPO (2019), https://www.wipo.int/publications/en/details.jsp?id=4386
161 Lauri Donahue, *A Primer on Using Artificial Intelligence in the Legal Profession,* JOLT DIGEST (Jan. 3, 2018), https://jolt.law.harvard.edu/digest/a-primer-on-using-artificial-intelligence-in-the-legal-profession.

changes can be mostly seen in the possible shift of the back then typical billable hours to a new value-based or fix-free agreement.[162] Further, since AI can work as a prediction model or create predictive data, there could be an increase in outcome-based billing, where the fees would be based on the success of a patent prediction outcome. Additionally, the type of role which might be needed for tasks that would be considered routine and/or repetitive might be simply handed off to AI and some entry-level roles might disappear, however, the integration of AI specialists, or data and technology consultants can be added in business structures to maintain job retention. With this, new training programs and relationships between the legal and tech teams would need to be created to assure cohesive and efficient work products.

With the increasing use of AI in legal practice, it is likely that the reshaping of various aspects of the legal industry will take place. While this brings opportunities for increased efficiency and innovation, it also poses challenges related to ongoing professional development and changing business structures. Legal teams that successfully navigate these changes may find themselves better positioned to meet client demands and remain competitive in a dynamic legal landscape.

---

162 *Id.*

Conclusion

And, in a twist that might tickle your sense of irony, this conclusion—singing praises to the harmonious partnership between patent attorneys and AI—was itself crafted by AI at the prompting of a patent attorney, no less. Yes, the very subjects of our exploration lent a "hand" in painting the vision of its future contributions. So, as you ponder the expanding role of AI in the world of patent law, remember: even the articulation of its potential comes AI-assisted, proving that we're not just talking the talk, but walking the walk... or, should we say, computing the compute?

As we draw the curtains on this exploration of artificial intelligence's impact on the practice of patent attorneys, it's a moment to reflect on the journey we've undertaken together. This book has been an odyssey through the realms of possibility, where AI does not stand as a challenger to the expertise and irreplaceable intuition of the patent attorney but as a powerful ally, augmenting their capabilities and ushering in a new era of efficiency and precision.

The narrative we've woven, rich with the potential of AI, underscores a future not of displacement but of enhancement. Patent attorneys, equipped with AI tools, are poised to navigate the complexities of intellectual property law with newfound agility. The landscapes of patent searching, drafting, prosecution, and opinion work have been reimagined, transformed into terrains where the synergy between human intellect and artificial intelligence brings forth unparalleled opportunities for innovation and protection.

In this future, the role of the patent attorney is not diminished but magnified. The fusion of their deep legal acumen with the analytical prowess of AI enables them to offer more to their clients—greater insights, faster turnaround times, and strategic counsel rooted in a comprehensive understanding of both the minutiae of patent law and the broader strokes of technological advancement.

As we conclude, let this book serve not only as a testament to the journey thus far but also as a beacon for the path ahead. The integration of AI into the practice of patent law is a voyage we are just beginning, one that promises to make patent attorneys not only better at what they do but also more indispensable than ever in the quest to protect the fruits of human ingenuity. The future beckons with the promise of partnership between human and machine, a collaboration that will redefine the boundaries of what is possible in the realm of intellectual property.

APPENDIX
Application of AI to IP Law

In the journey through this book, we've explored the intricate dance between the evolving landscape of patent law and the groundbreaking role of AI. While the main chapters have been meticulously crafted to provide a coherent narrative on the profound impact of AI on the practice of patent law, there exists a wealth of knowledge related to the impact of AI on IP law that, though invaluable, diverges from the primary storyline. It is with this understanding and appreciation for the depth and breadth of AI's influence that we present this appendix.

This supplementary section is dedicated to shedding light on the different aspects of AI, its development, capabilities, and its application to IP law from a broader perspective. While this content steps away from the direct application of AI in patent law, the importance of this information cannot be overstated. AI is not merely a tool but a paradigm shift in how we interact with technology, data, and even the concept of intelligence itself.

We offer this appendix as a resource, aiming to enrich your understanding of AI beyond its specific applications—to foster a comprehensive grasp of its potential and challenges. It's provided with the recognition that while it doesn't flow seamlessly with the primary focus of our book, the insights it holds are too significant to be omitted. Thus, we place this knowledge here, at the appendix, ensuring that this important and useful information is presented and not lost.

As you delve into this appendix, we encourage you to view it as both a conclusion and a continuation of the narrative—an exploration of the broader context in which the fusion of AI and IP law exists. It's a glimpse into the underpinnings of the technology that's poised to redefine our world, offering perspectives that, while tangential to our main discussion, are crucial for a holistic understanding of the AI revolution.

Welcome to this exploration of AI, a journey into understanding the technology that shapes our future, provided here to ensure that no valuable insight is left behind as we navigate the complexities of a world where law and technology converge.

LEGAL INNOVATION: THE ARTIFICIAL INTELLIGENCE REVOLUTION IN THE EFFICIENCY AND QUALITY OF PATENT RESEARCH, DRAFTING AND PROSECUTION.

According to what has been established above and having a clear idea about Artificial Intelligence and Patents, which have a correlative according to the new technologies.

Artificial intelligence (AI) tools have emerged as indispensable allies in the field of patent research, drafting and prosecution, revolutionizing traditional processes and catapulting efficiency to unsuspected levels. This marriage of science and technology not only accelerates development times, but also enhances the quality and accuracy of the results.

"AI could transform our world and the role it can play in using AI as an enabler of new methods, processes, management and evaluation in research" (Cyranoki 2019; UKRI 2021).[163]

First, the research phase benefits greatly from the massive data processing capabilities offered by AI tools. These platforms can analyze

---

163 Jennifer Chubb, Peter Cowling & Darren Reed, *Speeding up to keep up: exploring the use of AI in the research process*, AI & SOCIETY, 37(4), 1439–1457 (Oct. 15, 2021), https://doi.org/10.1007/s00146-021-01259-0.

huge scientific databases, identify patterns and relationships not evident to a human researcher, and generate detailed summaries of existing literature. In addition, AI is able to track technological advances at a speed that surpasses human capabilities, providing researchers with a more complete view of the current state of the art and thus a solid patenting foundation.

Scientific research has undergone a significant transformation in recent decades thanks to the continuous advancement of Artificial Intelligence (AI). This technological phenomenon has emerged as an invaluable tool that not only facilitates, but also enhances research capabilities, offering a range of benefits that redefine the way we approach data generation and analysis.

Artificial Intelligence has revolutionized information gathering. Using advanced algorithms, it is capable of processing large data sets in real time, allowing researchers to obtain more accurate and faster results. This increase in efficiency accelerates the pace of research, enabling significant breakthroughs in record time.

Additionally, AI has proven to be an invaluable ally in identifying patterns and correlations in complex data. The ability to recognize relationships not obvious to the human eye has led to fundamental scientific discoveries in fields ranging from medicine to quantum physics. AI acts as a catalyst for innovation, providing insights that might otherwise go unnoticed.

In the field of medical research, the subject of study has played a crucial role in analyzing large genomic databases. This approach has led to the identification of genetic markers linked to diseases, enabling more accurate diagnosis and the development of personalized treatments. Thus, AI becomes an indispensable tool for advancing the understanding and treatment of complex diseases.

On the other hand, the automation of routine tasks freed up by AI allows scientists to devote more time to experimental conceptualization and design. By delegating the repetitive workload to intelligent systems, researchers can focus on more creative and analytical aspects of their projects, fostering innovation and the generation of disruptive ideas. As Artificial Intelligence becomes more deeply integrated into scientific research, ethical and social challenges arise that require careful reflection. It is critical to establish protocols and regulations that safeguard research integrity and mitigate potential algorithmic biases. In addition, transparency in the use of AI in research is essential to build public trust and ensure that the benefits of this technology are accessible to all of society.

The adoption of Artificial Intelligence (AI) in the field of scientific research has experienced exponential growth in recent years. According to recent data from UNESCO, a large percentage of researchers around the world today incorporate AI tools in their projects, evidencing the rapid integration of this technology into the global scientific community.[164]

A clear example of the quantitative impact of AI in research is the significant increase in data processing speed. It is shown that tasks that would normally take months or even years can be completed in a matter of days thanks to machine learning algorithms and neural networks. This efficiency not only speeds up results, but also allows researchers to tackle more complex and ambitious questions.[165]

In addition, it is worth noting that the automation of tasks has led to a reconfiguration of researchers' time management. According to research conducted by the McKinsey Global Institute, science,

---

164 UNESCO, *El aporte de la inteligencia artificial y las TIC avanzadas a las sociedades del conocimiento: una perspectiva de derechos, apertura, acceso y múltiples actores*, UNESDOC, (2021), https://unesdoc.unesco.org/ark:/48223/pf0000375796.

165 *Usando inteligencia artificial para analizar datos no estructurados: imágenes, texto y voz*, WAVEBI, https://wavebi.com.es/noticias/inteligencia-artificial-y-el-analisis-de-datos-no-estructurados/.

technology, engineering, and mathematics (STEM) professionals will see a 16% increase in the proportion of their working hours automated, reaching 30% by 2030, as a result of the rapid adoption of Artificial Intelligence. This reorganization in the distribution of intellectual effort has led to a discernible increase in creativity and innovation within multiple activities, including research.[166]

In academia, Artificial Intelligence (AI) has proven its worth as a substantial tool for enhancing research productivity and excellence. A thorough analysis carried out by the Department of Computer and Systems Engineering of the University of La Laguna reveals that those academic institutions that integrate AI in their research processes experience a remarkable increase in both the number of scientific publications and in the citation of their research. This phenomenon only underlines the significant contribution that Artificial Intelligence can make to the advancement and effectiveness of applied research activity now within an academic environment.[167]

However, the rapid adoption of AI also poses challenges. A World Health Organization report highlights the need to address ethical issues related to privacy and data security, underscoring the importance of developing regulatory frameworks that safeguard the rights of individuals and ensure the integrity of research.[168]

In summary, Artificial Intelligence has left an indelible mark on the field of scientific research. Its contributions go beyond process improvement; it redefines the way we approach scientific problems

---

166 Eric Revell, *Accelerated adoption of AI could automate 30% of Americans' work hours: McKinsey,* FOX BUSINESS (Jul. 27, 2023), https://www.foxbusiness.com/economy/accelerated-adoption-ai-automate-30-americans-work-hours-mckinsey.

167 Carina S. González-González, *El impacto de la inteligencia artificial en la educación: transformación de la forma de enseñar y de aprender, Revista de Teoría,Investigación* Y Práctica Educativa. Universidad de La Laguna *(Jul. 2023), https://doi.org/10.25145/j.qurricul.2023.36.03.*

168 *WHO outlines considerations for regulation of artificial intelligence for health,* WHO, (Oct. 19, 2023), https://www.who.int/news/item/19-10-%20 2023-who-outlines-considerations-for-regulation-of-artificial-intelligencefor-health.

and accelerates progress toward discoveries that transform our understanding of the world. However, it is imperative to address the ethical and social challenges associated with its implementation, ensuring that AI is a positive and equitable force in the advancement of scientific knowledge.

In terms of patent drafting, artificial intelligence proves its worth by optimizing the creative process and ensuring completeness in drafting. Natural language processing algorithms can suggest technical terms and phrases, ensuring that the patent is drafted clearly and accurately. AI can also automatically verify the originality of the content, avoiding potential conflicts with existing patents and increasing the likelihood of acceptance by the relevant offices.

In the specific field of patent drafting, Artificial Intelligence (AI) presents itself as an invaluable ally by transforming and optimizing the creative process, ensuring the completeness and accuracy needed in this legal and technical field. Natural language processing algorithms play a central role in suggesting technical terms and phrases, helping patents to be drafted clearly and concisely.

The ability of AI to suggest specialized technical language not only streamlines the drafting process, but also improves the quality of the final document. These algorithms analyze prior patents, technical documents and field-specific terminology, offering contextual suggestions that enable drafters to efficiently incorporate the distinctive features of the invention in question. This approach not only speeds up drafting time, but also contributes to the consistency and clarity of the patented text. The ability of AI to suggest specialized technical language not only streamlines the drafting process, but also improves the quality of the final document. These algorithms analyze prior patents, technical documents and field-specific terminology, offering contextual suggestions that enable drafters to efficiently incorporate the distinctive features of the invention in question. This approach not only speeds up drafting time, but also contributes to the consistency and clarity of the patented text.[169]

Additionally, AI plays a crucial role in automatically verifying the originality of content. By analyzing vast databases of existing patents, AI can identify similarities and disparities, avoiding potential conflicts and ensuring that the proposed invention is unique and novel. This automated process not only reduces the likelihood of rejection by patent offices, but also provides an additional layer of legal certainty to the inventor by minimizing litigation risks related to the originality of the invention.

In terms of efficiency, AI not only speeds up the drafting and verification process, but also facilitates adaptation to constant updates and changes in patent law. Machine learning algorithms can continuously monitor and analyze updates in laws and regulations, ensuring that drafted patents comply with the latest requirements. This is essential in a constantly evolving legal environment, where accuracy and regulatory compliance are essential to the success of any patent application.[170]

The application of Artificial Intelligence in patent drafting is not only limited to the initial process, but also extends to the management and maintenance of patent portfolios. Intelligent systems can monitor changes in the legal status of patents, automatically alerting on expiration dates, renewals and possible legal conflicts. This automated management capability not only saves time and resources, but also reduces the risk of unintentional loss of intellectual property rights.

Despite the obvious benefits, it is essential to address the ethical

---

169   *AI-Powered Patent Search: Revolutionizing Intellectual Business Research*, LINKEDIN (Nov. 14, 2023), https://www.linkedin.com/pulse/ ai-powered-patent-search-revolutionizing-intellectual-business-exdaf.

170   Maurice Bretzfiled, *The Impact of AI on Intellectual Property Practices: Revolutionizing The Legal Profession* (Oct. 3, 2023), https://www.linkedin.com/pulse/ impact-ai-intellectual-property-practices-legal-maurice-bretzfield.

and legal challenges associated with implementing AI in patent drafting. Transparency in the use of algorithms, protection of data privacy, and fairness in access to this technology are key considerations that must be carefully addressed to ensure the integrity of the system and the trust of all stakeholders.

The integration of Artificial Intelligence (AI) in the field of patent drafting has led to remarkable and quantifiable results, with a significant impact on the efficiency and accuracy of the patent drafting process, which is of both legal and technical importance. According to recent analyses, there has been a substantial reduction in the time required for drafting patent applications through the implementation of AI. On average, the application of natural language processing algorithms has proven to be effective in decreasing the time spent on drafting, thus contributing to the acceleration of the pace of filing new inventions.

In terms of practitioner adoption, research reveals that a large number of IP attorneys are integrating AI tools into their patent drafting processes. This significant increase in adoption reflects lawyers' growing confidence in AI's ability to improve efficiency and quality in the preparation of complex legal documents.

As for the number of patent applications drafted with the help of AI, the figures are revealing. According to data from the World Intellectual Property Organization (WIPO), during the period from 2013 to 2016, 40% of patent applications filed globally incorporated AI algorithms, including some derived within the drafting process. This statistic underscores the rapid penetration and acceptance of AI in the intellectual property arena, highlighting its central role in the drafting of legal documents critical to innovation.[171]

---

171 World Intellectual Property Organization (WIPO), *The Story of Artificial Intelligence in Patents*, WIPO, https://www.wipo.int/tech_trends/en/artificial_intelligence/story.html (last visited Mar. 24, 2024).

The effectiveness of AI in ensuring originality of content is also reflected in acceptance statistics by patent offices. According to reports from the European Patent Office (EPO), applications drafted with AI assistance show a higher acceptance rate compared to those drafted in the traditional manner. This improved approval rate underlines the ability of AI to identify and avoid potential conflicts with existing patents, ensuring the uniqueness of proposed inventions.[172]

A World Bank study indicates that companies that incorporate AI into their patent drafting processes experience an increase in productivity, translating into tangible economic benefits. This direct correlation between AI adoption and economic performance supports the notion that the technology not only improves operational efficiency, but also contributes to economic growth in the area of intellectual property.[173]

On the other hand, the contribution of Artificial Intelligence to global economic growth is projected to be three or more times the current magnitude by 2030, in contrast to expectations for the next five years. The net global impact, estimated at $13 trillion in additional value compared to current global Gross Domestic Product (GDP), is likely to materialize over a longer period.[174]

It is imperative to highlight that, despite the obvious benefits, the ethical implementation of Artificial Intelligence in patent drafting remains a subject of debate and regulation. It will be necessary to analyze the impact of Artificial Intelligence on legal practice, as well as its ethical implications for legal professionals. The importance of addressing the ethical implications associated with the use of this technology is emphasized.

---

172 *Artificial intelligence*, EUROPEAN PATENT OFFICE (May 2, 2022), https://www.epo.org/en/news-events/in-focus/ict/artificial-intelligence.

173 Jacques Bughin, Jeongmin Seong, Janes Manyika, Michael Chui, & Raoul Joshi, *Notes from the AI Frontier Modeling the Impact of AI on the World Economy*, MCKINSEY&COMPANY (Sept. 2018), https://goo.su/DwGvpH.

174 *Id.*

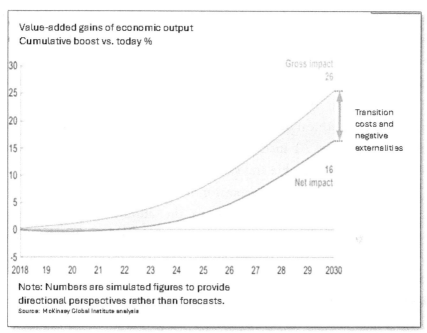

Value-added gains of economic output
Cumulative boost vs. today %

It is critical to note that the patent practitioner employing artificial intelligence tools must perform continuous verification of the accuracy of the results generated.[175] In addition, additional adjustments and edits are necessary to ensure that the content meets the requirements of the dynamic intellectual property landscape. Failure to verify the accuracy of artificial intelligence output has recently resulted in sanctions imposed on attorneys who filed court documents with false legal citations. Reference can be made to the specific case of Mata v. Avianca to show the legal consequences associated with this failure to verify.[176]

---

175 Gene Quinn, Anthony Prosser, Mark Vallone, Sivon Kalminov & John M. Rogitz, *The Ethics and Practicality of AI Assisted Patent Drafting*, IPWATCHDOG (Aug. 31, 2023), https://ipwatchdog.com/2023/08/31/ethics-practicality-ai-assisted-patent-drafting/id=166094/.

176 Mata v. Avianca, Inc., (2022), Justia Law.̈ https://law.justia.com/cases/federal/district-courts/

These statistics reveal an encouraging picture regarding the positive impact of Artificial Intelligence in the field of patent drafting. From reduced drafting time to increased acceptance rates, AI has established itself as a fundamental tool for professionals and companies seeking to optimize their IP processes. The challenge ahead lies in continuing to develop ethical and legal frameworks to guide the responsible implementation of AI in this context, ensuring that its benefits are maximized in an equitable and sustainable manner.

Artificial Intelligence has transformed patent prosecution by simplifying, accelerating and optimizing the administrative processes associated with intellectual property protection. From document management to communication with authorities and deadline tracking, AI has established itself as an essential tool that not only improves efficiency, but also minimizes human error, providing a significant boost to the likelihood of success in the patent prosecution process in an increasingly dynamic and innovative environment.

In short, the integration of artificial intelligence tools in patent research, drafting and prosecution not only represents a technological breakthrough, but also redefines efficiency standards in the field. By leveraging AI's data processing and analytics capabilities, practitioners can streamline their processes, freeing up time and resources to focus on innovation and the creation of new technologies. In a world where speed and precision are key, artificial intelligence is positioned as an indispensable ally on the road to scientific and technological progress.

The integration of Artificial Intelligence (AI) in the field of patent drafting has generated measurable transformations that directly impact the efficiency and effectiveness of processes. Examining concrete data reveals that the use of specialized algorithms in patent prosecution has

---

new-york/nysdce/1:2022cv01461/575368/54/.

demonstrated substantial reductions in waiting times.

Patent offices are increasingly embracing artificial intelligence (AI) because of its ability to analyze extensive data sets and deliver relevant results. According to the World Intellectual Property Organization (WIPO), more than 70 AI projects are underway in 27 offices, 19 of which are specifically focused on prior art searches and application examination procedures.[177]

Data compiled by WIPO reveals that the implementation of AI in patent offices has led to a significant reduction in patent prosecution times. This decrease not only benefits the speed of obtaining intellectual property rights, but also accelerates innovators' access to the market, thus fostering innovation and contributing to economic development. AI's ability to analyze millions of pieces of data efficiently translates into substantial improvements in the efficiency and effectiveness of IP-related processes. This innovative approach not only optimizes patent management, but also boosts competitiveness and expands opportunities for creators and entrepreneurs.

And in relation to the integration of Artificial Intelligence by professionals, it has been observed that IP attorneys have been incorporating and studying artificial intelligence tools in their activities related to patent prosecution. This increase in adoption reflects the lawyers' confidence in the ability of Artificial Intelligence to optimize processes, reduce timeframes and increase the quality of the documentation filed with the respective patent offices.

Regarding the incorporation of Artificial Intelligence (AI) by companies, the most recent statistics indicate that the proportion of companies adopting AI by 2022 has more than doubled since 2017. However,

---

177 Kathy Van der Herten, *AI proves effective at improving patent office efficiency and application timelines*, CAS (Mar. 23, 2022), https://www.cas.org/es-es/resources/casinsights/intellectual-property/ai-proves-effective-improving-patent-office-efficiency.

stagnation has been observed in recent years, with that proportion remaining in a range between 50% and 60%, according to results obtained from the annual research survey conducted by McKinsey.[178]

Organizations that have implemented AI report significant cost reductions and revenue increases. This increase in adoption reflects the confidence of professionals, including attorneys, in AI's ability to streamline processes, decrease time and improve the quality of documentation filed with patent offices. This confidence not only highlights AI's proven effectiveness in improving operational efficiency, but also underscores its crucial role in substantially improving document management, thereby contributing to business success and the effectiveness of IP-related procedures.

Undoubtedly, artificial intelligence has led to an appreciable decrease in the administrative burden that lawyers usually face in the field of patent prosecution. Specialized algorithms have demonstrated a remarkable capacity to efficiently manage the relevant documentation, rigorously follow up on established deadlines and facilitate effective communication with the corresponding authorities. This technological advance has made it possible for legal professionals to spend more time addressing strategic and analytical aspects inherent to their cases, thus enhancing their ability to offer quality services and excellence.

Efficiency in the management of deadlines is a vitally important aspect in the context of patent prosecution, and artificial intelligence has proven to be highly effective in this area. The implementation of automated systems for monitoring deadlines has led to a significant reduction in cases of missed deadlines, avoiding substantial delays and possible rejections resulting from failure to meet established deadlines. This phenomenon conclusively supports the positive impact of

---

178 *Artificial Intelligence Index Report 2023*, STANFORD UNIVERSITY (2023), https://aiindex.stanford.edu/wp-content/uploads/2023/04/HAI_AI-Index-Report_2023.pdf.

Artificial Intelligence on patent prosecution procedures.

The contribution of artificial intelligence is palpably manifested in various aspects, from the significant decrease in waiting times to the notable increase in the approval rate of applications. This data alone unequivocally underlines the effectiveness of artificial intelligence in optimizing processes, thus improving results in the legal and technical field of intellectual property. This phenomenon represents a far-reaching transformation that consolidates artificial intelligence as an essential tool to face contemporary challenges linked to the protection and promotion of innovation.

According to research carried out by the Chemical Abstracts Service (CAS) in collaboration with the National Institute of Industrial Property (INPI) of Brazil, a national decrease of 80% in delays associated with the processing of applications at the National Institute of Industrial Property (INPI) has been observed. This result significantly underscores the positive impact of the measures implemented, highlighting a notable improvement in the efficiency of the application management process at the INPI.[179]

In conclusion, while AI offers enormous benefits in identifying the state of the art, it is imperative to carefully address the associated risks. Human oversight, transparency in algorithms, bias management, and cybersecurity are crucial areas that must be considered to take full advantage of AI's potential in this field without falling prey to the risks inherent in its careless implementation. Thoughtfulness and a diligent approach are essential to balance innovation with responsibility in the use of artificial intelligence.

---

179 Kathy Van Der Herten, *La Sostenibilidad de las offices de patentes y el cometido de la inteligencia artificial*, OMPI (Jan. 2023), https://www.wipo.int/wipo_magazine_digital/es/2023/article_0001.html.

ETHICAL CONSIDERATIONS AND THEIR INFLUENCE ON THE DUTY OF PROFESSIONALISM

The integration of artificial intelligence (AI) into the process of drafting sections of a patent raises significant ethical challenges for attorneys, especially with respect to their duty of professionalism and responsibility to their clients and the legal system in general. First, the use of AI to generate or suggest sections of a patent does not relieve the attorney of his or her duty of oversight and review. While AI can provide efficient and optimized suggestions, the attorney is still responsible for ensuring the accuracy, clarity, and legal adequacy of the final documentation. Lack of human oversight could result in misinterpretations, material omissions, or even the submission of incorrect information, which could compromise the validity and effectiveness of the patent.

In addition, the lawyer has an ethical responsibility to understand AI suggestions at a deeper level. Blindly relying on AI recommendations without adequate knowledge of the underlying algorithms may result in acceptance of terms or formulations that may not be accurate, legal or ethical. Transparency into the workings of the algorithms is essential for the lawyer to be able to evaluate the integrity of the suggestions and make informed decisions.

The duty of confidentiality is also impacted when AI is used in patent drafting. Confidential client information may be subject to security risks, and the attorney must ensure that the AI systems used comply with rigorous cybersecurity and data protection standards.

In summary, while AI can be a valuable tool in the patent drafting process, attorneys should approach its integration with caution. The duty of professionalism involves active oversight, a thorough understanding of AI suggestions, and preservation of ethical and legal standards. Ethical reliance on AI requires a careful balance between leveraging its capabilities and assuming ultimate responsibility for the quality and integrity of the legal documentation.

Artificial intelligence (AI) is triggering significant transformations in various industries, including the legal field. However, its application raises fundamental ethical questions, particularly in relation to the obligation of professionalism that falls on lawyers.

The integration of AI into the drafting of legal documents, such as patents, can significantly improve efficiency and accuracy, but simultaneously raises questions about the duty of professionalism of lawyers. These professionals have a responsibility to provide competent services to their clients, which involves keeping abreast of changes in law and legal practice, including the adoption of relevant technologies.

The question of whether a lawyer can ethically rely on AI suggestions without a thorough understanding of the underlying algorithms turns out to be a complex issue. On the one hand, lawyers need not possess exhaustive knowledge of the inner workings of a technology to use it ethically; by way of example, lawyers get to employ computers and word processing software without requiring a detailed understanding of its underlying code.

On the other hand, however, it is essential for lawyers to have a basic level of understanding of how AI works in order to use it ethically. This does not imply the need to understand the precise technical aspects of the algorithms, but it does require a general understanding of the capabilities, limitations, and how training data can influence the results.

The incorporation of Artificial Intelligence (AI) in the legal field, especially with regard to patent-related issues, raises ethical issues that translate into relevant data that must be duly considered. One of the critical issues is the error rate associated with the use of AI in these specialized tasks. As legal professionals, it is imperative to perform a thorough analysis when employing these technologies, bearing in mind that, although such error rate may be minimal, there is always a percentage that must be considered to address possible eventualities arising from the use of these new technological tools.

According to an analysis conducted by the European Patent Office (EPO), it has been observed that the error rate in automated patent drafting has decreased significantly in recent years. Specialized algorithms have managed to reduce the incidence of errors to an impressive achievement, compared to that recorded in the early stages of technology implementation. This decline indicates a substantial improvement in AI's ability to generate accurate legal documents.[180]

However, despite these advances, there is a certain degree of skepticism among intellectual property lawyers regarding the absolute reliability of AI. This caution can be attributed to the inherent complexity of legal drafting and the need for contextual interpretation often expected of legal professionals.

In terms of the ethical perception of the use of AI in legal practice, an analysis carried out by UNESCO reveals that professionals such as lawyers consider the incorporation of AI in legal practice to be ethically acceptable, as long as clear protocols for its use are established and could even become best practices. This analysis reflects a significant openness to the adoption of emerging technologies, as long as the ethical standards established by the legal profession are respected.[181]

On the other hand, a large percentage of legal professionals have expressed ethical concerns regarding the safeguarding of data privacy when employing Artificial Intelligence in the patent application and prosecution process. This indicator highlights the imperative need to

---

180 *Artificial intelligence*, EUROPEAN PATENT OFFICE (May 2, 2022), https://www.epo.org/en/news-events/in-focus/ict/artificial-intelligence.

181 UNESCO, *El aporte de la inteligencia artificial y las TIC avanzadas a las sociedades del conocimiento: una perspectiva de derechos, apertura, acceso y múltiples actores*, UNESDOC, (2021), https://unesdoc.unesco.org/ark:/48223/pf0000375796.

effectively address the concerns inherent in the security and confidentiality of information within the legal arena.

The foregoing provides us with a nuanced view of lawyers' ethical reliance on Artificial Intelligence, especially in patent drafting and prosecution, which we discussed previously. Although the error rate has decreased markedly, there is a reservation on the part of some practitioners, and ethical concerns around data privacy still require attention. Striking an ethical balance in the implementation of AI in legal practice remains a critical issue as technology continues to evolve in this area.

In summary, while AI has the potential to improve legal practice, lawyers must employ it responsibly. It is critical that they stay informed about AI's capabilities and restrictions, while monitoring its use to ensure compliance with ethical and legal standards.

LEGAL CHALLENGES IN THE AGE OF ARTIFICIAL INTELLIGENCE: LIABILITY AND AUTHORSHIP IN PATENT PROSECUTION AND ARTISTIC CREATION

In the dizzying advance of Artificial Intelligence (AI), the question of legal liability emerges as an intricate labyrinth. In particular, when errors, oversights or failures in prior art knowledge impact crucial processes such as patent prosecution, the uncertainty as to who bears the burden of liability becomes a legal challenge of considerable proportions.

Against this backdrop, the crucial question arises: who, ultimately, is accountable for erroneous decisions or misunderstandings in the context of AI-assisted intellectual property? The developers of the technology, responsible for the creation and training of these systems? The law firm that, relying on the efficiency of AI-based tools, executed processes critical to the protection of intellectual property? Or perhaps, does the responsibility fall squarely on the patent attorney who, ultimately, is the legal guardian of his or her clients' interests?

In the search for answers, the complexity of the legal framework manifests itself. AI developers might argue that, although they have designed the technology, they cannot foresee all the possible applications and specific contexts of its implementation. On the other hand, law firms might argue that, by relying on cutting-edge tools, they are simply adapting to the demands of the modern legal environment, and that errors should be considered an inherent consequence of the process.

Meanwhile, the patent attorney, as the direct custodian of his clients' legal defense, faces the difficult task of discerning between his own responsibility and that of the technological tools he uses. To what extent can he delegate to AI and, at the same time, safeguard his professional integrity?

Current legislation does not offer such present answers, and precedents are scarce. The challenge lies in balancing the promotion of innovation and efficiency that AI provides with the need to establish boundaries and safeguards that mitigate potential legal risks. In this complex landscape, the legal community, technology developers and law firms must collaborate to establish clear ethical and legal standards that define responsibilities and protect clients' rights.

Ultimately, resolving the uncertainty around legal liability in the use of AI in patent prosecution will require a proactive and collaborative approach. Ethical reflection, transparency in AI-assisted legal processes, and clear delineation of roles and responsibilities are critical to ensure a future where innovation is not only driven by technological advances, but also supported by a robust and equitable legal framework.

The issue of authorship and the challenges associated with Artificial

Intelligence has generated a significant question mark in the doctrine and practice of scholars in this field. In particular, the central question arises as to who should be considered the author of a work generated through an artificial intelligence system.

LEGAL TRANSFORMATION: THE INTEGRATION OF ARTIFICIAL INTELLIGENCE INTO PATENT PRACTICE AND THE NEED FOR CONTINUING LEGAL EDUCATION

On the horizon of the technological revolution, the increasingly marked presence of artificial intelligence (AI) in legal practice, specifically in the field of patent prosecution, poses substantial challenges that require a proactive and robust response from the educational field. In this context, the continuing education of patent attorneys emerges as a key piece to ensure efficiency and ethics in a legal environment that embraces technological innovation. This analysis examines the intersection between artificial intelligence and continuing legal education, exploring how law schools and specialized courses must evolve to meet the emerging demands of an ever-changing legal practice.

In response to the increasing integration of AI, law schools must reevaluate and adapt their curricula to include training more prominently in artificial intelligence as applied to intellectual property. It is imperative that patent attorneys develop a thorough understanding of the technical intricacies of AI algorithms and, at the same time, acquire the ability to critically evaluate the results generated by these systems in a legal context.

THE EUROPEAN UNION'S ARTIFICIAL INTELLIGENCE LAW (8 DECEMBER 2023) AND ITS FUTURE IMPACT ON PATENT PRACTICE

December 8, 2023, marked a significant milestone in legislative developments related to artificial intelligence (AI) globally with the enactment of the European Union (EU) Artificial Intelligence Act, although the text still needs to be ratified before coming into force, which is expected to occur by the end of 2026, with some provisions coming into force earlier. This legislation stands out as the first comprehensive law on AI in the world, and its impact is not only limited to the ethical and regulatory aspects of the technology but will also influence key areas such as patent practice.[182]

The Artificial Intelligence (AI) Act represents a flagship initiative, with the potential to drive the development and adoption of safe and reliable AI in the European Union. This legislation proposes to regulate AI based on its capacity to cause harm to society, adopting a "risk-based" approach, where the higher the risk, the stricter the rules. As the first legislative proposal of its kind worldwide, the EU aims to establish a global standard for AI regulation in different locations around the world, somewhat similar to the impact of the General Data Protection Regulation (GDPR), thus promoting the European approach and pushing it forward on the global stage.

The context that led to the formulation of this legislation lies in the growing awareness that AI systems may threaten fundamental rights such as non-discrimination, freedom of expression, human dignity and privacy. In response, the EU has prioritized the development of

---

182 Jose Carlos Fernández Rozas, *The use of artificial intelligence in the EU will be regulated by the Artificial Intelligence Act, the world's first comprehensive law on AI,* EL BLOG DE JOSE CARLOS FERNANDEZ ROZAS (Dec. 9, 2023), https://fernandezrozas.com/2023/12/09/el-uso-de-la-inteligencia-artificial-en-la-ue-estara-regulado-por-la-ley-de-inteligencia-artificial-la-primera-ley-integral-sobre-ia-del-mundo-8-diciembre-2023/.

a human-centric approach to AI, ensuring that technologies benefit European citizens and adhere to EU values and principles.

The path to AI legislation began with the European Commission's 2020 White Paper on Artificial Intelligence, which called for the adoption of AI and the management of its risks. Initially, the Commission took an indicative approach, but evolved into a legislative approach, urging the adoption of harmonized standards for the development, commercialization, and use of AI systems.

In April 2021, the European Commission presented a legislative proposal that marked the first attempt to establish a horizontal regulatory framework for AI in the EU. This framework focused on the specific use of AI systems and their associated risks. The proposal sought a technologically neutral definition of AI, with a risk-based classification. Some AI systems deemed unacceptable would be banned, while others of "high risk" would require compliance with requirements and obligations to enter the EU market.

The Council and the European Parliament, after substantial negotiations and amendments, agreed on a position in December 2021 and the Parliament voted on the position in June 2023, respectively. The negotiations resulted in significant changes, such as revising the definition of AI systems, expanding the list of prohibitions, and imposing additional obligations on Member States.[183]

Main Elements of the Agreement:

The final agreement covers several aspects to ensure effective regulation of AI in the EU:

---

183 Jose Carlos Fernández Rozas, *The use of artificial intelligence in the EU will be regulated by the Artificial Intelligence Act, the world's first comprehensive law on AI,* EL BLOG DE JOSE CARLOS FERNANDEZ ROZAS (Dec. 9, 2023), https://fernandezrozas.com/2023/12/09/el-uso-de-la-inteligencia-artificial-en-la-ue-estara-regulado-por-la-ley-de-inteligencia-artificial-la-primera-ley-integral-sobre-ia-del-mundo-8-diciembre-2023/.

1. *Definitions and Scope:*
   - The definition of AI is aligned with OECD criteria.
   - Exclusions for areas outside the scope of the EU and without affecting national security competences.
   - Exceptions for exclusive military or defense use, research and innovation, and non-professional use.
2. *Classification of AI Systems:*
   - Horizontal protection layer, including high risk classification.
   - High risk" systems subject to specific requirements and obligations.
   - Prohibition of certain AI systems, such as cognitive manipulation and emotion recognition in workplaces and educational settings.
3. *Exceptions and Application of the Law:*
   - Safeguards for police use of AI systems.
   - Use of remote biometric identification subject to specific conditions and safeguards.
4. *Governance:*
   - Creation of an AI Office to oversee advanced models and promote standards.
   - Independent scientific panel to advise on GPAI models.
   - Participation of member state representatives on the IA Board.
5. *Penalties:*
   - Fines proportional to the overall annual turnover for violations.
   - Limits provided for fines to SMEs and new companies.
6. *Transparency and Protection of Fundamental Rights:*
   - Assessment of the impact on fundamental rights before launching high-risk systems.

- Registration requirement for public entities that use high-risk systems.
7. *Innovation Support:*
   - Measures to create a favorable framework for innovation and testing in limited, real-world environments.
   - Provisions to alleviate the administrative burden for smaller companies.[184]

European legislation seeks to establish an ethical and legal framework for the development and deployment of AI. In the following, we propose to briefly address how these legislative provisions could impact within the Patent Practice:

1) Categorization of AI Systems: The law classifies AI systems into various categories, from high-risk systems to low-risk systems. This has direct implications for patent practice, especially in terms of the evaluation and regulation of AI-related patents, which would be considered high-risk.

2) Transparency and Oversight: The need for transparency in the operation of AI systems is emphasized, as well as the implementation of oversight mechanisms. This could have implications for the documentation and disclosure of AI-related patents to ensure a clear understanding of their operation.[185]

3) Liability and User Rights: The law establishes clear principles of liability and user rights in relation to AI. This could influence the contractual provisions associated with AI patents and the obligations of patent holders.

---

184 Jose Carlos Fernández Rozas, *The use of artificial intelligence in the EU will be regulated by the Artificial Intelligence Act, the world's first comprehensive law on AI,* EL BLOG DE JOSE CARLOS FERNANDEZ ROZAS (Dec. 9, 2023), https://fernandezrozas.com/2023/12/09/el-uso-de-la-inteligencia-artificial-en-la-ue-estara-regulado-por-la-ley-de-inteligencia-artificial-la-primera-ley-integral-sobre-ia-del-mundo-8-diciembre-2023/.

185 *Proposal for a REGULATION OF THE EUROPEAN PARLIAMENT AND OF THE COUNCIL amending Council Regulation,* EUR-LEX, https://eur-lex.europa.eu/legal-content/EN/TXT/?uri=CELEX%3A52018PC0368.

In analyzing the potential impact of the new law on Patent Practice, it is noted that the classification of artificial intelligence (AI) systems according to their level of risk implies a more thorough, but beneficial assessment of AI-related patent practices. Those innovations considered high risk could face additional scrutiny during the patent process. In addition, the transparency requirement could have an impact on patent filings, as applicants would have to provide detailed information on the implementation of AI in their innovations, thus facilitating evaluation by patent authorities. The law stresses the importance of ethics in the development and use of AI, which translates into an ethical evaluation of AI patent applications, especially in inventions with significant ethical implications and of which have been assisted by AI. This ethical approach not only affects the approval or rejection of patents, but also sets an ethical standard for the community of innovators, encouraging more responsible practices in the field of artificial intelligence.

This groundbreaking legislation seeks not only to encourage technological advancement, but also to ensure that the development and implementation of artificial intelligence is conducted in an ethical and socially responsible manner. In the context of AI patents, the law introduces specific mechanisms to assess not only the novelty and technical applicability of an invention, but also its potential ethical ramifications.

With the advent of this Act, patent applications related to artificial intelligence should now be subject to a rigorous ethical review process, analyzing the possible social consequences, the impact on individual and collective rights, as well as any potential risks to security and privacy. This approach would make us recognize that technological innovation cannot be separated from its ethical and social implications, especially when it comes to powerful tools such as artificial intelligence.

Taken together, these points point to a potential shift in the dynamics of Patent Practice in the field of AI, where risk assessment, transparency and ethical considerations could become key elements during the patent application and review process. This evolution only reflects to us the adaptation of intellectual property regulations to the ethical and safety demands associated with emerging technologies, such as Artificial Intelligence.

The EU Artificial Intelligence Law will represent a pioneering framework, and its impact will continue to evolve. Adapting patent practice to these regulations requires a continuous understanding of the changes and flexibility to adjust to future updates, where collaboration between the legal community, industry and patent agencies will be essential to ensure effective and ethical implementation of these IP regulations.

As we move toward a future where AI plays a central role, adapting to regulations, such as those established by the European Union (EU), becomes essential. These regulations not only define the legal framework for intellectual property, but also establish guidelines on ethics and responsibility in the development and application of AI technologies. Reminding us about the balance between innovation and responsibility and that technology should be a means for the common good, respecting ethical and fundamental values. As we move forward in this new era of AI regulation, may our creativity always be focused on ethical awareness and the pursuit of progress that benefits all. The pursuit of progress should not only be driven by efficiency and competitiveness, but also by a commitment to development that benefits all of society.

GLOBAL INTELLECTUAL PROPERTY IMPLICATIONS: ARTIFICIAL INTELLIGENCE IN PATENT PRACTICE AND ITS JURISDICTIONAL NUANCES

As we have previously mentioned, it is essential to address the global implications of intellectual property in the context of artificial intelligence (AI) as applied to patent practice. In a world where innovations transcend borders, the integration of AI raises questions that resonate across jurisdictions. Globalization calls for examining how different countries regulate the use of AI in the legal arena, especially in patent protection and prosecution.

The perspective on the use of AI in patent practice varies across jurisdictions. Some nations are quick to adopt AI for its benefits in efficiency, accuracy and speed, while others are more cautious, highlighting ethical and safety concerns.

Some jurisdictions have taken proactive stances toward AI-driven technological transformation in patent practice. Investments in continuing education and technology reflect commitments to intellectual property adaptation and innovation. The significance of this issue is evident in the words of Vladimir Putin, who warns that "the country that succeeds in leading the development of artificial intelligence will be the master of the world".[186]

In the case of Mexico, the regulatory landscape of AI is constantly evolving. Legislative initiatives stand out, such as the Bill for the Ethical Regulation of Artificial Intelligence and various proposals for AI regulation, including copyright for works generated by algorithms.[187]

---

186 *Which countries dominate artificial intelligence and what are their national strategies?,* PUENTES DIGITALES (Aug. 13, 2018), 018/08/13/ que-paises-dominan-la-inteligencia-artificial-y-cuales-son-sus-estrategias-nacionales/.
187 *An initiative is promoted to enact the Law for the Ethical Regulation of Artificial Intelligence and Robotics,* CAMARA DE DIPUTADOS (May 27, 2023), https://comunicacionsocial.diputados.gob.mx/index.php/boletines/

The beginning of the regulatory framework in Mexico dates back to 2018, when the country submitted resolutions 72/242 and 73/17 to the United Nations (UN) [188]. These initiatives marked the beginning of a significant debate at the international level on the global impact of Artificial Intelligence. The diversity of proposals reflects Mexico's intention to grant an ethical and legal regulation of AI, addressing ethical, criminal and intellectual property aspects to encourage its responsible development.[189]

The attitude towards the use of artificial intelligence in patent practice varies considerably between jurisdictions. While some actively embrace technological innovation, others take a more cautious and ethical approach, thus generating a diversity of perspectives that influence the future evolution of AI in the legal arena internationally.

In this context, jurisdictions leading in the adoption of artificial intelligence in patent practice are expected to experience tangible benefits in terms of efficiency, speed and accuracy in IP-related processes. Effective implementation of AI can enable rapid and accurate patent identification, novelty assessment and eligibility determination, significantly streamlining the IP lifecycle. However, more cautious jurisdictions will continue to play a crucial role in insisting on consideration of fundamental ethical and legal issues. Discussions around transparency, fairness and accountability in the use of artificial intelligence in the patent arena will become even more relevant in this evolving landscape.

Ultimately, the future of artificial intelligence in international patent practice will depend on the ability of nations to collaborate effectively, sharing knowledge, experience, and best practices. This

---

impulsan-iniciativa-para-expedir-la-leyde-regulacion-tica-de-la-inteligencia-artificial-y-la-robotica.

188   *The regulation of Artificial Intelligence in Mexico*, COLEGIO JURISTA (Sept. 13, 2023), https://www.colegiojurista.com/blog/art/la-regulacion-de-la-inteligencia-artificial-en-mexico/.

189   *Accelerating Artificial Intelligence Regulation: Mexico and Other Countries at the Forefront*, MAYA COMUNICACION (Nov. 28, 2023), https://mayacomunicacion.com.mx/acelerando-la-regulacion-de-la-inteligencia-artificial-mexico-y-otros-paises-a-la-vanguardia/#google_vignette.

collaboration will not only optimize efficiency in the patent system but will also ensure that the adoption of artificial intelligence in this context evolves in an ethical and equitable manner, thus preserving the fundamental principles of intellectual property in the digital age.

As an epilogue, we leave you with the following reflection:

"The inevitable integration of artificial intelligence into patent prosecution reminds us of the importance of critically addressing the ethical, legal and economic challenges of this new era."